The Letter from James

CHOICES

from Deception to Blessing

James Schuppe

SHENANDOAH PRESS

SHENANDOAH JCT, WV

Library of Congress Control Number: 2020904741

ISBN: 978-1-7346385-1-6

Printed in the United States of America

DEDICATION

This book is dedicated to the memory of the man who led
me to Christ at the age of seven, George A. Miles,
President of the Washington Bible College.

CONTENTS

ACKNOWLEDGMENTS

This book owes its origin to wonderful times I had as a professor in the classroom with my students at the Washington Bible College. Their penetrating questions caused me to dig deeper to find answers that weren't in the standard answer collection. I'm grateful for all the students at WBC and sad that the school is no more.

I am grateful to George A. Miles, a civil engineer for the government who became President of the Washington Bible College. He was one of my instructors when I entered the college at the age of seventeen. He hired me as a full time teacher when I was twenty-four and became a close friend as I worked with and under him for twenty three blessed years. He was an excellent Bible teacher with amazing insight which enabled him to evaluate situations and people with uncanny accuracy. Thanks "Uncle George."

I owe a large debt of gratitude to my beautiful wife of fifty years, who has put up with a rather flaky, sometimes blind-to-what's-important husband. She is an amazing woman of God, joyful in the Lord, faithful in service, compassionate toward those in need, a wise counselor, and most of all, she loves me and thinks I'm hot stuff! Thanks Martha.

Chapter 1
The Challenge of Being "Scattered"

*"James, a bondservant of God and of the Lord Jesus Christ,
to the twelve tribes which are scattered abroad: Greetings"*
—(James 1:1)

You would think that the first verse would be the easiest verse to skip. After all everyone knows that there are twelve tribes in the nation of Israel and that they've been scattered from time to time. And everyone knows that James is a bondservant of God because he is writing a book in the Bible. The sentence is nothing more than James' saying "hello."

But there are words which appear kind of odd. For example, why would James choose to address "twelve tribes" instead of "the saints who are in Ephesus," or some other town? Is he writing to Jewish people more than Gentiles? And why does he mention "scattered?" Is there something special about the location of his readers? Did James intend to include tribes that weren't scattered? And which "James" is this? Weren't there two disciples with that name?

When you think about it there are several questions that arise. I want to address five of them because of the impact they have on our understanding of the letter.

I. The Author Was James

The author identifies himself but doesn't narrow the field enough. Which James? It looks like there are four candidates at least as far as Scripture is concerned.

A. James the son of Alphaeus was a disciple (Matthew 10:3; Acts 1:13), but we don't know much about him. He may have been Matthew's brother (also the son of Alphaeus Mark 2:14). He could have been the writer, but there is little information on him, and he doesn't do much talking in the Gospels.

B. James the father of Judas the disciple wasn't a disciple himself (Luke 6:16; Acts 1:13). The chances are slim that he would be the writer.

C. James the son of Zebedee, was one of the sons of thunder along with John, who authored five New Testament letters – the Gospel of John, 1, 2, and 3 John, and Revelation. Could John's brother James write as well as he did? Probably yes, and he would be a good candidate for author except that he died quite early. He was martyred by Herod in AD 44 (Acts 12:1-2). If he wrote the epistle, it would have to have been written early.

D. James the step-brother of Jesus. Jesus had at least four step-brothers, and a couple of sisters (Mark 6:1-3). His brothers apparently did not believe in Him during His lifetime (John 7:5). But somewhere along the line they realized who their brother was and turned to Him as their Savior.

As a result, right after Jesus ascended into heaven (Acts 1:9-11), the disciples assembled in the upper room. Here's the list of people that were there:

> And when they had entered, they went up into the
> upper room where they were staying: Peter, James, John,
> and Andrew; Philip and Thomas; Bartholomew and
> Matthew; James the son of Alphaeus and Simon the
> Zealot; and Judas the son of James. These all continued
> with one accord in prayer and supplication, with the
> women and Mary the mother of Jesus, and with His
> brothers. (Acts 1:13-14)

The interesting addition is, "and with His brothers." That statement tells us that a change had taken place between John 7:5 and Acts 1:14. The brothers had turned to Christ! James even had a private meeting with Christ after His resurrection (1 Corinthians 15:7).

Soon after that event, James became a leader in the church. Peter said, "go, tell these things to James and to the brethren" (Acts 12:17). By Acts 15, when the first church council assembled, James made the concluding judgment in verses 13-21, to which the rest of the council agreed. By Acts 21:18 James seemed to be the leader of the church. He and Peter were the first apostles Paul visited in Galatians 1:18-19. Most Bible students view this James, the step-brother of Christ, as the author of our letter.

But perhaps it was written by James the son of Zebedee, the brother of John, who was martyred in AD 44. Why should we consider him as a possible author? Because of the statement, "to the twelve tribes which are scattered abroad."

II. The Twelve Tribes

Why would James address his letter to "the twelve tribes" instead of the church of Jesus Christ? Addressing the letter to the twelve tribes suggests that the intended readers were all Jewish. Some have suggested that the title, "twelve tribes" is a title for the entire church composed of Jews and Gentiles. That may be so. But if James actually meant, "the twelve tribes," he would have had to write the book *before very many Gentiles had entered the church.* After that time, James couldn't have addressed the church as, "the twelve tribes scattered."

When the church began in Acts 2 it was composed entirely of Jewish people. Representatives from fifteen different locations are listed who heard the gospel for the first time from the apostle Peter. They were all Jews and proselytes (Acts 2:9-11). A proselyte was a Gentile who had been admitted into the nation of Israel by going through a process of (a) circumcision for males, (b) a purification of self-baptism in the presence of witnesses, and (c) offering a prescribed sacrifice.[1]

From Acts 2 through 7 a large number of people turned to Christ. On the day of Pentecost there were three thousand believers (Acts 2:41). Shortly after the number rose to five thousand (4:4). Then "multitudes" were added to the church (Acts 5:14). And they were all Jewish.

As the church grew persecution grew, Jewish leaders persecuting Jewish brothers who had trusted in the Jewish Messiah, Jesus. It started with threats (4:21), then the public stoning of a church deacon named Stephen (7:54-60). Then a radical Jewish leader named Saul, who had been part of Stephen's stoning, set out to imprison or kill the rest of the believers.

One of the major effects of the persecution was that the gospel spread to Gentiles. When Saul made things too dangerous in Jerusalem, some of the people went over to Samaria (Acts 8:1-4). The Samaritans were looked down on by Jewish people as being only part Jewish. But some of these "half Jews" turned to Christ and received the Holy Spirit (8:6, 17).

Then an Ethiopian eunuch turned to Christ (8:36-38). He was probably a proselyte who feared God and had visited Jerusalem in order to worship at one of the great festivals. But then in Acts 10 Cornelius, a genuine Gentile, turned to Christ (10:44-48). By Acts 11:19-26 a large group of Gentiles in the area of Antioch had turned to Christ.

At first Jewish people were reticent to preach Christ in front of Gentiles, but almost accidentally, the message came to them:

> Now those who were scattered after the persecution that arose over Stephen traveled as far as Phoenicia, Cyprus, and Antioch, preaching the word to no one but the Jews only. But some of them were men from Cyprus and Cyrene, who, when they had come to Antioch, spoke to the Hellenists, preaching the Lord Jesus. And the hand of the Lord was with them, and a great number believed and turned to the Lord. (Acts 11:19-21)

Apparently the standard method was to announce the gospel to Jews only. But some believers didn't know any better and preached the Lord Jesus to the Hellenists (Greeks). And surprise, "a great number believed and turned to the Lord." This event in Acts 11:21 was the beginning of a *non-Jewish* wing of the church. Before this time the entire church could have been addressed as the *twelve tribes*.

The result was that these persecuted Jewish refugees became the first Gentile missionaries, perhaps not intentionally, but in spite of their discouraging circumstances. You can see how simple it all was. Gentiles would meet them and ask, "why are you here in our town?"

Their response would be something like, "because I was forced out of Jerusalem." Then when asked to explain the story they would naturally want to talk about their Messiah, Jesus Christ.

III. The Twelve Tribes Were "Scattered"

The fact that James includes the word "scattered" suggests that he wrote *after* the persecution began in Acts 8 and *before* very many Gentiles had come to Christ. The word *scattered* pictures sowing seed in a field by tossing it randomly. It usually refers to Jewish people *outside of Palestine* scattered throughout the Gentile world, sometimes *by force*, being deported by various conquerors, and other times *by choice*, maybe for business reasons, or to escape famine.

But this scattering was motivated by the hate of a radical Jewish Pharisee named "Saul":

> Now Saul was consenting to his [Stephen's] death. At that time a great persecution arose against the church which was at Jerusalem; and they were all scattered throughout the regions of Judea and Samaria, except the apostles. And devout men carried Stephen to his burial, and made great lamentation over him. As for Saul, he made havoc of the church, entering every house, and dragging off men and women, committing them to prison. (Acts 8:1-3)

Havoc is a strong word. Think of what this experience did for young believers who had turned to Christ for forgiveness and peace. They expected a life of fullness and joy, but instead found *great persecution* and *havoc*. As a result, thousands of them left Jerusalem and went, "throughout the regions of Judea and Samaria." They weren't intending to leave Israel, but by the time Saul was finished only the apostles were left in town. Some didn't even stop at the borders of Israel but "traveled as far as Phoenicia and Cyprus and Antioch" (Acts 11:19).

These people may have lost their homes, or lands, or jobs, and were now perhaps temporarily settled. Life for them had become upset; it wasn't the way it used to be. The challenges arose *because they turned to Christ.* If they had remained normal unbelieving Jews, Saul the persecutor would not have bothered them and they would still be living in the comfort of their homes in Jerusalem.

Think of the questions they would have: "didn't Christ promise to meet all of our needs? Why all this pain and frustration? Is this what the Christian life is supposed to be? Or are we doing something wrong? Maybe this is punishment. Maybe we shouldn't have left our Jewish heritage." Perhaps the overall question was "why has the Lord allowed this to happen to us?" And the follow up question might be, "how are we to respond to this strange kind of unsettled life? What does God want us to do? And when will He get us out of this stress and back to living a normal life?"

Some people choose to become refugees. My grandparents voluntarily left Russia in 1912 to come to America, hoping to begin a new life here. And they did. But these people had made no such plans; they simply and suddenly were scattered by a violent man named Saul.

And they weren't the first. It's surprising how often refugees appear in the Bible. Abraham, for example, was a foreigner in the land of Canaan and lived in tents for one hundred years (Genesis 23:4-6). The nation of Israel was enslaved in Egypt, and God later on reminded them to treat foreigners graciously because they knew what it was like to be a foreigner (Deuteronomy 10:17-20; 16:10-15; 24:14-22). Moses himself was a "sojourner in a foreign land" (Exodus 2:21-22). Ruth was a refugee in Israel (Ruth 2:10-11), Esther was a foreigner in Persia, Daniel and Ezekiel were captives in Babylon. And Jesus Christ was the greatest refugee, coming to earth as an insignificant carpenter.

News of this sudden explosion of Gentile believers came back to Jerusalem, and they sent Barnabas down to Antioch to help. As a result many more people turned to Christ (Acts 11:22-24).

The divine irony of it all was that the man who came to encourage these scattered Jewish believers as well as their new

Gentile believer friends was the very man *who had started the scattering* in the first place, Saul of Tarsus! He had turned to Christ (Acts 9:1-9) and was now team-teaching "a great many people" with the veteran, Barnabas (Acts 11:25-26).

Thus by Acts 11 we see probably the first non-Jewish church. Saul and Barnabas were developing the first inter-racial worship of Christ the Jewish world had ever seen. And it was this group of largely Gentile believers in the city of Antioch that received the new, probably derisive title, "Christians" (Acts 11:26).

If James did indeed write at this time he wrote to people in the middle of changes that brought difficult challenges along with amazing blessings. And their difficulties arose *because they were Christians, because they were special to God.*

The problem was that no one else seemed to understand their special status. Others saw them as insignificant, as a bother, as people who didn't fit. Their special relationship with God was part of the reason they had such problems. If God didn't have such big plans for them they wouldn't be in so many difficulties. Here they were, visitors, misunderstood, ignored, and **God seemed to want it that way.**

IV. What Motivated James to Write?

If the scenario drawn above is correct, James wrote to help young Jewish believers sort out the problems their scattering had brought. The fact that Acts 11:24 gives us the first wave of Gentile believers into the church of Jesus Christ suggests that this epistle was written soon after. Otherwise James would not be able to address only twelve tribes.

The early date of this epistle also suggests the tone we see in it. James seems to be influenced by two people, Jesus and Judas. The influence of the Sermon on the Mount and other messages by our

Savior comes out in statements like, "let your 'Yes,' be 'Yes,' and your 'No,' 'No'" (5:12 and Matthew 5:37), and "this man shall be blessed" (1:12 and 1:25 with Matthew 5:3), and "be doers of the word, and not hearers only" (1:22 and Matthew 7:24-27). The letter clearly shows that happiness and holiness in life only come from obedience to Jesus Christ.

But James also seems to be greatly affected by the example of Judas Iscariot. I'm sure you have experienced unforgettable events that have shaped your life. If you were more than a child on 9/11 when the twin towers came down, you were probably permanently shaped by the unfolding horror of that day. It was so fearful, unbelievable and unforgettable, that it distorted your thinking for days and weeks and years after. Some events are so life-changing we never get beyond them.

Our twenty-two-year-old son died in 2005. You would think that by this time we would "get over" that tragedy. But no, that event changed our lives permanently.

Imagine being at the last supper with Jesus and the other eleven disciples, and watching the fellowship abruptly change when Jesus announced that one person in the room would betray Him. With everyone on pins and needles, wondering if He was referring to them, a mysterious interaction between Jesus and Judas unfolded. It ended when Judas left.

But it didn't end. Three hours later Judas re-appeared as a totally different person. He had sold out to the enemy, a group that had one goal, to kill Jesus. Think of watching Judas be transformed into a demon. He was a respected disciple. His peers looked up to him. That's why they elected him treasurer. To think that someone they trusted that much sold the very Messiah of Israel was mind boggling. How could he?

I doubt the disciples ever got over the shock and pain of that betrayal. They probably re-lived their years with Judas in light of that act, and never stopped analyzing his actions and statements. I'm sure the question Judas asked in John 12:5 took on a different light, "why was this ointment not sold for three hundred denarii and given to the poor?"

As they rehearsed those three plus years with Judas they perhaps could see his slide downwards from lying to deceiving to becoming a professional hypocrite, and being able to talk convincingly about what he didn't believe. He couldn't care less about the poor. John's commentary on this statement of Judas, sixty years later, was, "He said this, not because he cared about the poor, but because he was a thief, and having charge of the moneybag he used to help himself to what was put into it" (John 12:6). But at the time the disciples probably thought he spoke out of a heartfelt concern for the poor.

What would that betrayal experience do to James? I'm sure it made him much more cautious about his own deceptive tendencies, and much more insightful of those tendencies in others. Perhaps one of the things that motivated him to write was the realization that individuals in the church were going in Judas' direction, oblivious to the danger of their increasing deception and hypocrisy.

Out of the pain of Judas' example, James writes, "do not be *deceived,* my beloved brethren" (1:16), and "be doers of the word, and not hearers only, *deceiving* yourselves" (1:22), and "if anyone among you thinks he is religious, and does not bridle his tongue but *deceives* his own heart, this one's religion is useless" (1:26).

His fear arose out of a recognition of the normal human tendency toward relaxation and passivity. People who seriously want to live for Christ can go through their daily activities without really listening and obeying. They can read the Bible, study and talk about it, without actually getting hold of the truth they find and the changes it commands. This, James says, is like gazing into a mirror, seeing dirt on one's face, but doing nothing about it.

James may be writing with a vision of Judas playing up to Christ, acting like he was serious, talking a good line. It may be the ghost of Judas we see in chapter 2 when the usher seeks to impress the rich and ignore the poor (2:3); or in the man who speaks encouraging words to the poor (2:16) while doing nothing to help them; or in the demon's ability to affirm in emotion-laden tones his steadfast belief in God (2:19).

Perhaps Judas appears again in chapter 3 with the mouth that pours out both fresh and bitter water (3:11). He spoke great truths and boasted great things (3:5, 14), but his tongue was a fire, lit by hell (3:5-6) that ignited forests and left in its bitter envy and self-seeking wake (3:14) confusion and every evil thing (3:16).

Perhaps he could see Judas in chapter 4 stirring up coveting and fighting and warfare and even murder (4:1-2). Maybe he was even the source of the controversy in Mark 10:41-45, and again at the last Supper in Luke 22:24. He could talk down others (4:11-12) and project his future plans with arrogance (4:13-17). He was covetous, collecting gold and silver (5:2-3), even at the expense of condemning and murdering "the just" (5:6).

Can you see James writing this letter with haunting visions of Judas in each section? He was still angry for allowing himself to be taken on a three year ride of deception by such a demonic disciple. At the same time he was alarmed to see children of God making decisions that mimicked Judas more than Jesus.

If this picture is in any way accurate it suggests that James was writing out of distress and pain, perhaps even fear. His letter wasn't simply a collection of aphorisms as some have suggested, sort of like the Proverbs of the New Testament. It wasn't storytelling or classroom education. Rather it was James doing what his last verse describes, turning "a sinner from the error of his way," saving "a soul from death" and covering "a multitude of sins" (5:20).

That's why we see an urgency in the form of fifty four commands in one hundred and eight verses. James is calling out, "do it!" "Don't become hearers only, do it" (1:22)! "Don't just talk about your faith, do it" (2:14-26)! "Don't just talk to others about how to live for Christ, change yourself" (3:13)! "Get afflicted and mourn and weep over your sins" (4:9)! "Cleanse your hands and purify your hearts you double minded"(4:8)! "Humble yourselves" for crying out loud (4:6, 10)! "Weep and howl" for the miseries that are headed your way (5:1)!

It was an urgency that came out of fear – fear that if nothing happened soon his readers would end up with souls being deceived to death (1:15, 21; 2:14; 5:20) like Judas.

If this description is in any way correct, it leaves us with the following conclusions:

(a) James was written by the disciple James, the brother of John, one of the sons of thunder, who died by the year AD 44 (Acts 12:1-2). He was one of the three closest friends of Christ (Peter, James, and John).

(b) James the brother of Jesus (the one normally assigned as writer) was not a disciple and didn't even believe in his step-brother during His ministry (John 7:5). Even though he knew and was affected by Judas' treachery, he didn't know Judas the way the apostles did. It's true that he grew rapidly after his conversion and quickly became a leader in the church, but if the letter was written before AD 44, it would seem that he wasn't ready for the task.

(c) The letter was written shortly after the dispersion of Acts 8:1-4 and 11:19-21 when the church was composed of Jewish people. If the first verse is to be taken seriously, it must have been written before very many Gentiles turned to Christ, or at least by the first missionary journey of Paul and Barnabas (Acts 13:1-4). That would make the letter very early. Some have suggested a date as early as AD 34 or 35.[2] If James actually wrote that early, his unforgettable experiences with Judas were less than five years old!

(d) Probably the letter was written later than AD 34-35 because of the condition of the readers. It takes awhile for a group of people to develop the tendencies James describes, becoming critical and unthankful, talking against and fighting with each other, impatient and covetous. The danger was that they were becoming like their Fathers in Numbers 11-14 or Isaiah 40:27 who had a great start in Christ but were losing their confidence.

Thus I wouldn't be surprised if James, the brother of John, finished this letter in AD 44, the night before Herod had him arrested and killed in Acts 12:2.

V. How Did James Organize His Letter?

Chapter one introduces three major challenges present in the life of every believer, *Trials, Temptations* and *God's Word.* Everyone faces these three big movers and shakers. Blessing comes from handling them properly.

Then in 1:26-27 James creates three examples of these movers and shakers at work in real life: (a) how *our inner conversation* affects us; (b) how we respond to *less significant people*; and (c) how the *pull and influence of the world* turns us.

The rest of the book discusses these six items at work, trials, temptations and God's Word coupled in sometimes unusual ways with the way we talk to ourselves, our relationships with less significant people and the pull of the world system, all in a context of deception.

Chapter 2 for example discusses our interaction with insignificant others (the poor) in light of how we speak to ourselves and become spotted by the world, by thinking that the rich man is going to benefit us more than the poor man. Chapter 3 emphasizes how our tongues guide us for good or bad, even how they become weapons against others (3:14-16). Chapters 4:1-5:6 emphasize how the world spots us with its temptations to use our tongues to get our way, cut down others, and promote ourselves.

Chapter 5 finishes what James started in 1:3-4, the declaration that all these difficulties are beneficial. They cause our growth when we obey the Word. The commands in 5:7-12 are an expansion of the initial thought of 1:4: "be patient in the middle of all your confusion, endure these things by doing what God's Word says, and you will love the outcome." Whether we can see it or not, God is using all of these things in majestic ways to make us "perfect and complete, lacking nothing."

The theme of the book appears in chapter 1: "but be doers of the Word, and not hearers only, deceiving yourselves" (1:22). The tension that appears throughout is between becoming a doer or becoming deceived. It's the tension between following Christ or following Judas.

I have outlined the book in a "challenge/deception" pattern. For example the first section (2-12) presents the challenge of handling one's trials properly so as not to be deceived into thinking they are your enemies. The challenge is in becoming a doer of the Word. The deception comes from lack of obedience.

What was James' **goal** for his readers? It all boils down to 1:12 , 1:25 and 5:11: "Blessed is the man . . ." and "this man shall be blessed . . ." and "we count them blessed who endure." James wants to pronounce "Shalom" on his readers as they find the source of God's blessing. The blessing is not automatic, but comes from God's approval of us in the middle of our challenges as we obey His Word.

And what does James mean by *blessing*? He covers that in 1:12. And what about disobedient children who don't get blessed? He covers that in 1:15 and 22, as well as 2:9 and 11. How does this blessing show up in our lives? James one covers that. Read on.

Chapter 2

The Challenge of Trials
(and the deception that views them as enemies)

James 1:2-12

The key verse that fences our thoughts in this chapter is verse 22: "But be doers of the word, and not hearers only, deceiving yourselves." This verse claims that there is a significant difference between listening and doing, a difference so huge that those who listen without doing mislead themselves and carry themselves astray. The word for "deceiving yourselves" actually means "to count wrongly," "to add things up incorrectly." If we don't listen closely, *we fail in life's math*. We misjudge what's important and talk ourselves into buying worthless trinkets in life.

Every person has been given a life that includes a generous amount of capital. We can spend that capital on valuable things that enhance our lives and society and glorify God by advancing His kingdom. Or we can waste that capital on junk stuff and wind up with a junk life.

God's desire is that we spend our capital in such a way that He can say of us, "this one will be blessed in what he does" (v. 25). What's the difference between being blessed by God and counting wrongly? It's enormous. And apparently that huge contrast can be experienced by *Christians*. James is not contrasting believers with unbelievers. He's talking about the possibility of *believers going the wrong direction by failing in life's math!*

And what makes for this difference? It's not the Bible because both people in verse 22 are *hearing*. The non-doer is listening to God's Word. "Doer of the Word" is the key phrase that distinguishes between the blessing of God and going astray.

What does it mean to be a "doer of the Word?" James is concerned that his readers don't understand the concept. People usually ask, "do what? do acts of good? pray? give money? Have a transcendent thought? Support a missionary?" And when you talk about *doing*, people automatically think of obeying the Ten commandments. Is that what James is talking about?

There is a difference between doing *good things* and doing *the Word*. This chapter introduces three major issues in everyone's life that determine whether one becomes a doer, *trials*, *temptations*, and *God's Word*. He introduces trials in the first twelve verses, temptations in the next eight (13-20), and the Word of God in the last five verses (21-25). Each is a challenge, and each involves the probability of deception.

Then in the last two verses (1:26-27) James introduces three examples we often overlook (bridling the tongue, visiting orphans, and keeping oneself from being spotted).

The first question is, "how do we become doers of the Word when we fall into various *trials*?" Verse two introduces the subject: "My brethren, count it all joy when you fall into various trials." In this section James gives *six commands to guide our thinking about how to do the Word*. Each command guides our response to various trials.

I. Command # 1 – Thank God for the Trial

My brethren, count it all joy when you fall into various trials,
knowing that the testing of your faith produces patience
(James 1:2-3).

A trial is an accident, a difficulty, a challenge that enters your life, usually unexpectedly, and *forces you to make a choice.* The hot water heater quits, your car won't start, your fifteen-year-old gets arrested, you lose your job, a tree falls on your house. James uses the word *various* to include many different colors and kinds. They all force us to make a choice; we cannot *not-* respond. We've got to say something, do something, hit something, react in some way – yell, scream, cry, kick, go to bed, leave the scene, *or thank God for it.*

A. Choose to focus on the *purpose* of the trial. Don't dwell on the pain or difficulty, but the *reason* for it. God's reason is in verse 3: it's a test of your faith and it will work patience in your heart. It's an educational experience; it's school from God's perspective. And His goal is *good,* to help us, even push us to grow. That's why He wants us to *count it all joy.* Counting it joy means choosing to view it from God's perspective. It's a friend; not an enemy.

That's not easy to do, especially when the trial makes it look like God has abandoned you. Remember that James is writing to "the twelve tribes . . . scattered." They were traveling, wandering, looking for some place to settle down, probably frustrated over the pain of it all. They had trusted Christ as their Messiah, become part of the new work of God, the church, saw amazing things happen, with thousands of people getting saved. But now they were facing loneliness, unsettledness and loss because of their testimony for Christ. All of a sudden they had few connections, and little position or authority.

At the same time as members of the twelve tribes they were the "elect" of God. That should have been comforting. But as Jewish people outside their land, they faced rejection by Gentiles. They sort of expected that. But as *Christian* Jewish people they were now rejected and persecuted by other Jewish people. That made for double whammy rejection. They needed comfort and encouragement.

But James doesn't really sympathize with them. He doesn't say, "I know you have it hard." Instead he wants them to choose God's outlook: *"do you know what is going on, do you understand what God is doing? He is giving you an opportunity to GROW!"* There is something more important than your pain; it's your maturity, your holiness, and that's what God is working on.

The word, *patience* introduces us to the heart of the issue. Why does growth take so long? For some reason maturity does not appear out of the blue, perfectly finished the first time we ask for it. There are delays, sometimes major delays, and we wait, and pray, and persevere. The truth is that by its very nature, patience can only be learned in the heat of trial, frustration, and exasperating conditions.

This epistle was written to people who were *in-between*. They had experienced the grace of God making them a child of God, but "patience" had not yet achieved its "perfect work," and they were not yet, "perfect and complete, lacking nothing" (1:4).

B. How you choose to respond indicates what you believe.
Job's wife said to him after all ten of their children died, and he was suffering from awful sores, "Curse God and die" (Job 2:9). She didn't believe that God was in control, or that God could bring anything good out of such a situation. She was telling her husband to put a tag on his trials: "they are from God and are *bad*." "Curse God." Job's response was, "the Lord gave, the Lord took away, blessed be the name of the Lord." Then it says, "he worshiped" (Job 1:20-22). That's the kind of response James is talking about.

When we say, "oh no, not again;" or "why me?" Or "why now?" Or "this is miserable?" Or, "I hate this life," "I see no hope," we demonstrate our *unbelief*. That sounds like Job's wife, "curse God and die." Unbelief views a trial as the enemy.

The truth is that a trial is the doorway to blessing. Verse 12 says that God wants to use this trial to bless you, those around you, and even the world through your response.

Back in 1967 Joni Eareckson (Tada) went on a family picnic to Sandy Point beach, on the Chesapeake bay. She dove into shallow water, broke her neck, and has been a helpless quadriplegic ever since. That was a life-changing trial. In her book *Joni* she talks about how she contemplated suicide. She felt hopeless after weeks of being strapped to a rigid bed. At one point she talked to her helper, Jackie, about giving her an overdose of pills or slashing her wrists.

One day, after just cussing out Jackie for dropping a fan and making too much noise, her boyfriend, Dick, walked in and read this to her: "When all kinds of trials and temptations crowd into your lives, my brothers, don't resent them as intruders, but welcome them as friends! Realize that they come to test your faith and to produce in you the quality of endurance" (James 1:2-3 from the Phillips translation).

After realizing the truth of this verse, she prayed, "Lord Jesus, I'm sorry I haven't been looking more to You for help. I've never thought of my accident before as something for testing my faith. But I can see how that's happened . . . Thank You for this lesson. With Your help, I'm going to trust You. Thank You that even this accident works together for good. I pray that others around me will see You through me . . ."³

Can you imagine that kind of prayer from a sixteen-year-old who could hardly move a muscle in her body? Maybe that's part of the reason God has used her to write more than forty Christian books and draw hundreds of pictures with a pen held between her teeth, make a full length feature film, record records, speak for Jesus Christ in more than thirty-five countries around the world, be a member of Billy Graham's Lausanne conference on Evangelism, be on the board of five missions, and have a radio program heard on more than one thousand outlets!

Joni is a doer of the Word. It started with a completely life-altering event that shut down all her plans and dreams. Now more than fifty years later we can see the word *blessed* in Joni's life.

That trial in your life is something *good*. It's a *friend* in disguise. It may not feel good, it may not look good, but *God says that it is good*. He has creatively designed it to strengthen your faith. Are you going to believe Him – and rejoice in it and thank Him? Or are you going to trust your senses, trust how you feel at the moment, and abhor a friend bringing blessing to you? Your first choice determines whether you are blessed by God, or deceive yourself and miss the purpose of the trial.

II. Command # 2 – Go Through the Trial Fully

Knowing that the testing of your faith produces patience. But let patience have its perfect work, that you may be perfect and complete, lacking nothing (James 1:3-4).

"Let patience have its perfect work" is an interesting command. How do you "let?" Does this mean, "give patience *permission* to do its work?" It could mean that. Does it mean, "don't *hinder* patience from its work?" Yes, perhaps. But it's stronger than that. James is saying, "this needs to happen," "this must happen," "you've got to make sure that this various-trials process completes its work." Why?

A. Trials make us grow. We say to children, "grow up" because we want them to realize that their present childish behavior should be temporary. God's goal is, "that you may be perfect and complete." That's why we face so many trials. God wants us to grow up. Verse 4 says that His goal is "perfect and complete." The word *perfect* doesn't mean, "sinless," but rather, "mature," or "trained." The truth is that *God has plans for us to become holy.*

The problem is that some kids don't like the process, and are determined to get out of it, to quit, to duck the difficulties. Can you remember perhaps back in the fourth grade, when you were assigned to give an oral report in front of the whole class on, let's say, "building igloos in Alaska?" Somehow you developed a massive stomachache the morning you were supposed to speak and couldn't go to school. You had to lie in bed with a hot water bottle on your stomach.

What was that? You were ducking the trial. You didn't like the process and were inventing another way. If you had a wise mother, she figured it out and sent you to school! Fourth grade is one thing, but it's far more serious to repeat those same choices in attempting to duck God's school of life. Such behavior leads to deception.

That's why the command is, "let patience have its full work;" "make it happen;" "you'll like what it accomplishes."

B. Growth depends on doing it God's way. The command is to let patience have it's *perfect work.* You don't want partial credit here. You can't join God half-heartedly. You want it *all.* After all, since His plan is perfect, since His desire is for our best, why would you want to miss anything He has? Why would you want only one day of a scheduled one month vacation in Hawaii? The trial is God's way of giving you the vacation in Hawaii.

The truth is that it doesn't *feel* that way when you face a difficulty. It's hard to picture a severe trial as a vacation in Hawaii. We only begin to see it in its proper perspective afterward, and sometimes, long afterwards. The writer to the Hebrews understood this contrast when he penned, "Now no chastening seems to be joyful for the present, but painful; nevertheless, afterward it yields the peaceable fruit of righteousness to those who have been trained by it (Hebrews 12:11).

"Afterward" is the key. "For the present" chastening is "painful." But afterward it bears "the peaceable fruit of righteousness" as we become trained by it!

Think of a nice big beautiful, white mushroom. Where do mushrooms like that grow? To grow so purely white, you would expect it to grow up in a white atmosphere. At least a clean atmosphere. But no, mushrooms need *dirt* in order to grow. And even though the mushroom started as a small plant in the middle of a large amount of dirt, none of that dirt gets into the mushroom. You can eat a mushroom and taste none of the grittiness, nothing but pure mushroom taste.

That's how God works. The dirt represents the difficulties, frustrations and chaos in life, things that don't look clean or holy or Godly at all. They don't look capable of producing anything remotely approaching pure adulthood. But God, in the middle of the dirt, wants to bring you out as something totally different, a mature, holy, faithful, joyful, fruitful, adult who loves Him with all your heart. What a picture!

Thus the encouragement in verse four is, "don't run away," "don't try to get out of this difficulty," "don't leave the family," "don't run from the church," "don't give up." Re-evaluate what is happening. Perfection, maturity is the destination and perseverance is the only way to get there.[4]

III. Command # 3 – Ask God for Wisdom

> *If any of you lacks wisdom, let him ask of God, who gives to all liberally and without reproach, and it will be given to him (James 1:5).*

Why would anyone need wisdom? If they've decided to go through their difficulty God's way that's exactly what they need. The first question that arises after agreeing with verse four is, "what should I do now?" "What should I say or not say?"

What is your response when an impossible situation jumps into your life and stops you in your tracks? Do you think you should you read a book? Go to counseling? Go to school? James' command is, **ask!** "Ask, and you will be impressed with the response of your God. Ask, and you will meet your God in a new way."

There are three striking descriptors of God in this verse: "who gives to all liberally and without reproach, and it will be given to him."

First, when you ask you will realize that your God is liberal. He's liberal in His gifts. He supplies wisdom all around to everyone who asks. It seems that most Christians believe that their God is conservative, perhaps even a little tight. That attitude makes us hesitant about asking. James wants us to ask of a liberal giver!

Secondly, our God does not reproach. "Reproach" is the word, insult, or revile, scold, in the sense of throwing it back at us and saying, "haven't you asked enough, go find your own wisdom." God never gets tired of hearing our problems, getting another emergency request at midnight for wisdom as to how to handle our sick child. He loves hearing from His children no matter what the situation is.

Thirdly, James states matter-of-factly that God will give us wisdom: "It will be given to him." "Will be" is future passive. The passive voice suggests that we don't have to do anything. It's done to us! This is God saying, "you ask, you don't have to do anything else, it will be there." I have been amazed many times at how quickly and clearly answers come when I stop what I am doing to ask God for wisdom.

Aren't those amazing statements of God? Do you believe them? God wants to introduce Himself to us in perhaps a new way, as a liberal giver, as One who doesn't reproach, or insult, or get tired of our requests, as One who delivers what He promises.

That's one of the reasons for our problems: God wants us to meet Him. A trial is an opportunity to understand God in a new light. Have you prayed for wisdom in your latest trial? You have to literally stop trying to work it out as best you can, turn to God, and **Ask!**

IV. Command # 4 – Ask in Faith

But let him ask in faith, with no doubting . . . (James 1:6).

Perhaps you are thinking, "yes, here's the real crunch point: we shouldn't get too positive about verse 5 until we fulfill verse 6." God gives liberally, and doesn't reproach, and it will be given him. Yes, *but only if one asks in faith.*

So everything in verse 5 hinges on verse 6. What does it mean to ask in faith? Is it even possible for unfaithful people like us to ask in faith? Perhaps that's why requests have come back unopened, unanswered. Maybe that's why we feel so alone in circumstances. Maybe we're not asking in faith.

But what is faith when we face difficulties? The answer is very simple. *It's not a feeling.* I used to think that faith was a feeling, and that I had to have some kind of totally confident feeling in God before I made a request. So I would try to talk up my confidence and whip up a mood of really believing God, then quickly make my request before the mood died out.

That's not what James is talking about. Faith is not a feeling. Faith is an action. It's a decision to believe God and do what He says, *no matter how I feel.* "By faith Noah *moved* with godly fear, prepared an ark" (Hebrews 11:7). "By faith Abraham *obeyed* when he was called to go out and he went out" (Hebrews 11:8). "But as many as *received* Him, to them gave He power to become the children of God, even to them who believe on His name" (John 1:12).

For Noah, faith was building an ark; for Abraham, faith was leaving his home to find God's city. For an unbeliever, faith is receiving Christ as Savior.

What is faith when facing trials? It's obeying verses 2 through 5. It's asking for wisdom *in order to count it all joy*. It's asking for wisdom *because you have determined to go through the trial the right way*. It's your commitment to God's program of growth coupled with the realization that you will only obey these commands with God's wisdom. So you turn to Him for answers and the ability to do it right. That's faith.

Faith says, "I'm going to believe God when He says that all things work together for good to those who love Him. And I'm going to respond the right way to this trial; I'm going to count it all joy and determine to go through it to get all the benefit out of it." Faith says, "I need wisdom to do this without messing it up. I'll get it from God. He has it and will share it generously." That's *a doer of God's Word*. It doesn't depend on how you feel. It depends on whether you choose to obey what God says rather than what you can see and feel. Our responsibility is to *ask in faith*.

V. Command # 5 – Don't expect God to respond to a faithless request

> But let him ask in faith, with no doubting, for he who doubts is like a wave of the sea driven and tossed by the wind. For let not that man suppose that he will receive anything from the Lord; he is a double-minded man, unstable in all his ways (James 1:6-8).

Faith is such a critical component of our requests for wisdom that James adds three more verses to emphasize the nothingness of faithless prayers.

Instead of faith it is possible to be "double-minded." The picture in verse 6 is of one who wobbles, or waves, like a wave of the sea that is "driven and tossed by the wind." A double minded person goes in two directions. One direction believes what God has promised. The other direction believes what he can see. He hasn't made up his mind yet.

It's like Peter walking on the water. He had the promise and command of Christ, who said "Come." He stepped out of the boat by faith in Christ's word. He obeyed. But when he started looking at the storm and the size of the waves he probably started thinking, "what am I doing here? I'm going to kill myself!" And he started to sink (Matthew 14:25-32).

He cried out, "Lord save me." Jesus immediately stretched out His hand, caught him, and asked, "O you of little faith, why did you doubt?"

Peter was double minded. He had great faith in stepping out of the boat onto nothing but water. None of the other disciples were interested. But his faith was distracted by the noise and chaos of the waves. He started with obedience to Christ's word. But when he got into the wind and the waves, he stopped focusing on the words.

It's possible to "obey" verses 2-5 with your fingers crossed, waiting to see what's going to happen, wondering whether you should back out if God doesn't come through. That's double-mindedness. And that person will not find the help he needs to succeed. In fact, James says in verse 7, "I can promise the double-minded person one thing: nothing. He will go through his trial alone."

Maybe verse 7 contains the reason why some of our prayers are not answered. We're not sure about our God, and we're not sure we want to commit ourselves fully to God's design. James says, "count it all joy," "determine to get it fully," and "ask God for wisdom."

VI. Command # 6 – Rejoice in Your Status Change

> *Let the lowly brother glory in his exaltation, but the rich in his humiliation, because as a flower of the field he will pass away. For no sooner has the sun risen with a burning heat than it withers the grass; its flower falls, and its beautiful appearance perishes. So the rich man also will fade away in his pursuits. Blessed is the man who endures temptation; for when he has been approved, he will receive the crown of life which the Lord has promised to those who love Him (James 1:9-12).*

The sixth command in this section is to *glory*, or *boast*, to *take pride in*, to *rejoice*, or to *be glad*. Why would God command us to boast? I thought He was against pride and boasting. The answer is that trials *change our status*. They introduce us to God's wealth by adding us to the *blessed* category. And that's something to be proud of.

A. Every trial is the evidence that God is at work. It shows us that He is doing something God-like with us. Every trial changes your status. It exalts the lowly person, and humbles the rich person. Both of those adjustments are for our good.

"Rich" or "lowly" probably represent the stamp that others put on them. Because one drives a Rolls Royce or lives in a larger house others may view them as *rich*. Because one walks everywhere and serves as a high school janitor, the community stamp may be, "poor." Of course the stamp may be completely wrong. The "rich" may be up to his neck in debt; the "poor" may be out of debt and serving others. The rich may look like he has something to offer. He's looked up to, respected in the community, appears on TV to make statements on the state of global warming. The poor seems to be overlooked in most of those areas.

The point is that external details tend to mislead. The rich begin viewing themselves as solid, stable trees. The poor may look at the privileges of the rich and feel they have been overlooked and are less significant.

Trials enter our lives to equalize these cultural misunderstandings. When a hurricane floods the mansion of the rich and puts his Rolls under water it helps him view himself realistically, like grass. And that's good! Rather than depending on his riches for blessing, he needs to realize that God wants to give him a life of blessing, with or without the riches. Like Job, he needs to say, "blessed be the name of the Lord" (Job 1:21).

On the other hand, the term "lowly brother" speaks of a person who doesn't rise far in life. He may be ignored and overlooked. No one recognizes what he does, no one calls seeking his advice, no one even invites him to a banquet, much less to speak at it.

In what are the poor and rich to boast? What is their "exaltation?" It's the attention and presence of the Lord. It's the obvious love of the Lord, for "whom the Lord loves, He chastens" (Hebrews 12:6). The trial is the chastening.

Both need to realize that they can enjoy the greatest life possible on earth because they are children of God, no matter what their physical circumstances promise. Trials are God's instruments to help people get off their cultural rose colored glasses and view their lives truthfully.

We are to boast in the fact that God is opening the door for us *to grow up!* Chances are good that someday we will look back on this difficulty as a turning point in our lives. Get ahead of the game and glory in its importance now. Every trial, every temptation, every problem can strengthen and mature us when we find and obey God's wisdom. One thing is for sure; we will never stay the same.

B. Every trial is specially designed to bless us. The wrong view sees trials as things *to get over*, get out of, in order to get on with life. The right view sees *trials as our life, our joy, our blessing.* Trials are not just additions, they are the journey; *they are the life!* "Happy is the man who is right now in the middle of a trial and is enduring," verse 12 instructs. He may not feel happy, he may not look happy, but he will find that the trial was not an interruption as much as the pathway to life.

Gene Walter was an eighty-year-old man mentioned in Luella Nash LeVee's book *Pure Joy* who received a diagnosis that said, "inoperable brain cancer with probably less than six months to live." A year and a half later he gave this testimony: "the most wonderful thing that ever happened to me in my spiritual life is to come down with cancer because it opened up the Word of God."[5]

I find it fascinating that Gene did not say, "how wonderful it was to get healed of my cancer because then I could go back to living." Instead it was the cancer itself that opened up his life to real living through the Word of God. That's what James is saying: "this impossible trial you are facing is going to do more for your spiritual life than you ever dreamed possible!"

Look at the beginning and end of verse 12 – "blessed is the one enduring trials," and "to those who love Him." It's one thing to love God when He gives you what you want. It's a brand new thing to love God when He gives you what is difficult and painful.

Have you ever been there? That's a radical perspective on life. *Trials are the doorway to life!* Most people miss the doorway, or go right past it, or slam the door shut, because they don't understand the awesomeness of what God is doing.

Verse 12 introduces two different kinds of blessing: "for when he has been approved" is the first part and speaks of God's *intention* in the trial; He wants to put His stamp of approval on our lives. It's what the teacher does after you have aced an exam.

If it sounds a little too human for God to want to stamp an "A" on the life of His child, think about how He described Job: "And the LORD said to Satan, 'Have you considered my servant Job, that there is none like him on the earth, a blameless and upright man, who fears God and turns away from evil?'" (Job 1:8).

Do you catch the attitude? He seemed proud of the fact that Job was mature, upright, feared Him, and turned from evil. He seemed happy to make that announcement to Satan saying, "here's one of my men; look at him!" Maybe God wants to say the same thing about us as we succeed our trials. He wants to approve us.

The second part of God's blessing comes at the end of verse 12: "he will receive the crown of life which the Lord has promised to those who love Him." The "crown of life" is not a heavy, golden halo placed on your head so you can strut around in eternity. Think rather about a *mark of honor*. The crown was "the wreath or garland which was given as a prize to victors in the public games."[6]

What happened when someone received the wreath that signified victory in the games? It's intrinsic value may not have been much, but it signified that the receiver had reached the ultimate, the summit of life in terms of the games.

That pictures James' thought here. He's not talking about a kingly crown, but a crown for victory, which results in the peak, the ultimate of life – *the kind of life that everyone is looking for!* Enduring difficulties God's way results in the ultimate kind of life – the *blessed life!* **Trials are the doorway to the ultimate life that everyone is looking for.**

James wants his readers to understand where God's blessing originates. He doesn't say, "*after you get over all this*, then it will be good." Rather he's talking about "the rest of your life" *right now*. God wants us to meet Him in the middle of the difficulties and uncertainty, with the unanswered "why" questions still unanswered.

James declares, "blessed is the person who right now is enduring temptation."

It's not an issue of *waiting* until everything gets straightened out, quieted down, easy to work, that we then live the genuine Christian life. These pressures, these quandaries, these unsolvable issues **ARE the Christian life!** That's where we find grace that meets our needs. That's where we find strength to endure what cannot be endured. And *in this process* we meet and become like God.

Some of you who are reading this are more blessed than you think. That's why verse 9 calls you to glory in your status. God may have you in the greatest time of your life. Perhaps you're not enjoying it because you don't trust Him.

Are you a *doer of the Word*? Becoming a doer involves six commands:

1) View the trial as something good; thanking God for it.

2) Determine to go through it fully and get everything God wants you to get out of it.

3) Ask God for wisdom to make the right choices.

4) Ask in faith, meaning, "ask in order to obey Him."

5) Don't think that asking apart from faith will result in anything more than silence.

6) Glory in the status God has graciously given you by this trial.

God is bringing difficulties and painful things and hard situations into our lives – not to hurt us at all, but to do what nothing else can do – to help us grow to be like Him. Amazing? Don't miss it. *Trust* Him and *thank* Him and *determine* to go all the way thru it with Him, and *ask* Him for His wisdom.

Chapter 3
The Challenge of Temptations
(and the deception that assumes they are friends)

James 1:13-20

Verse 13 introduces a different outcome in trials. The first section ended with the possibility of a life of *blessing*. But verse 15 ends with the word, *death*. Verse 12 pronounces the *crown of life* on the person "who endures temptation." But verse 15 introduces the possibility of death – even for "my beloved brethren" (v. 16). It's as if brethren face life or death possibilities in each trial.

Verse 13 has the key phrase, "tempted by evil." Verse 2 introduced us to "various trials" of different colors and kinds. But now the focus is on one specific type of trial, a temptation to *evil*.

What does it mean to be a doer of the Word when tempted by evil? Section one directed how we talk to ourselves about our trials and difficulties. "Thank God for them," "determine to go through them," "ask God for wisdom," "ask in faith" and "rejoice in your status change."

But now the issue is how trials can turn into temptations, how we process offers from the other side. This is the negative side – becoming a doer of the Word by *not talking yourself* into doing this list of things.

Several years ago a young woman in a trench coat walked up to the door of a police station in Iraq and asked if she could come in and get her wallet which she had left there the day before. When the attendant at the door refused, she blew herself up and injured two people in the building. Imagine living in that kind of culture where you are faced with choices that could kill you immediately.

The reality in James 1:13-20 is that *we live in that kind of culture.* And the one who comes dressed up as the cute young woman asking to enter, is Satan himself or one of his demons. His desire is to blow up our lives so we experience "death." How does he get into the door of our hearts? Verse 16 says it's **by deception.** I find in this section **five well-used arguments** that repeatedly deceive us and open the door for the cute young terrorist to come in, loaded with explosives:

1) "God made me this way and I can't help it."

2) "The devil made me do it."

3) "It's not going to kill me."

4) "The devil always seems to make the best offers."

5) "I don't need any help."

The answers to these five deceptions (and many more) are in God's Word. We only find them as we obey verses 19-20 and become quick to listen, slow to speak, and slow to anger.

I. "God made me this way and I can't help it"

> *Let no one say when he is tempted, "I am tempted by God"; for God cannot be tempted by evil, nor does He Himself tempt anyone (James 1:13).*

The addition of "by evil," helps define this type of trial. The Greek word "to test" can also mean "to tempt." They are often opposite sides of the same coin. We distinguish the two by the form of allurement. A simple way to think about it is, "a temptation is what I *like* but *should not do*. A testing is what I *don't like*, but *should do*." Mint Chip ice cream is a temptation. Cod liver oil is a test.

This distinction helps us understand Genesis 22:1. The King James Version says, "God did tempt Abraham." That's confusing when our verse (1:13) says that God does not tempt anyone. Did He tempt Abraham? What did God ask him to do? He asked him to offer his son, Isaac, as a sacrifice. Was that something he *wanted* or *didn't want to do?* It was a "test," not a "temptation" because he had no interest in doing that. The New King James helps clarify the word by translating, "God tested Abraham."

The question here is, "how do we blame God for our temptations?"

A. We view ourselves as victims. "I just can't help it; it's the way I am built." "It's my environment, my boss, my husband, my parents, my neighbors, my children, the dog, the thermostat." "They are such a problem and make life difficult. If I could just get out of my present environment and into a better one."

Think about that line of reasoning. If a better environment would make you better, what if you were in a *perfect environment?* Would that make you really good? Maybe we should talk to Adam and Eve, because they started in a perfect environment, and from *there* they fell into sin. What went wrong? Their environment? No, it was something inside them, which disproves the victim theory.

In contrast, when Jesus Christ was in the wilderness for forty days with nothing to eat, He didn't fall. Environment didn't help Adam even though it was perfect, and didn't hurt Christ, even though it was awful. Everything Adam needed for happiness was in the Garden of Eden; very little that our Lord needed was in the wilderness. And yet Adam fell the first time he was tempted, while Jesus never sinned even though He was tempted again and again.

Some people say, "well it's just my nature." "I'm ambitious, I want to get the job done; I am in a hurry. That's why I'm cutting corners, or peoples' throats." Others say, "I'm a perfectionist; I've got to have it right; I'm obsessive about exactness, so shut up and get out of here." Or, "why did God make me with these uncontrollable desires? Why was I created with such a need to eat? Why am I so attracted to sex? Or to succeed? Or to be popular?" Or, "why did my parents abuse me?" All of this is ultimately blaming God.

B. Adam and Eve viewed themselves as victims. It wasn't long after Adam and Eve sinned that God found them hiding and asked, "why were you hiding?" They said, "we were afraid because we were naked." God said, "Who told you that you were naked? Have you eaten from the tree of which I commanded you that you should not eat" (Genesis 3:10)?

That was the question: "have you eaten of the tree?" What was the answer? Do you remember their answers? Both of them "confessed." Adam said, "I ate" in Genesis 3:12, and Eve said, "I ate" in the next verse. But notice how they couched their confessions.

Here's Adam: "The woman whom You gave *to be* with me, she gave me of the tree, and I ate." What's he saying? Is he admitting guilt? Well, yes, but it's really the woman. "You know if it hadn't been for the woman who handed the fruit to me and put it in front of my nose and ate a bite herself in my face, and almost stuffed it down my throat, I might not have done it. But, yes I ate."

"And remember You gave her to be with me. Perhaps if You had not brought her into my life, to hand it to me and put it in front of my nose and eat a bite herself in my face, I might not have done it. Yes, I ate, but I couldn't help it."

OK, so much for that clear confession of guilt. Here's Eve's "confession" in the next verse: "The serpent deceived me, and I ate." What's she saying? Is she admitting her guilt? Well, yes, but it's really the serpent. "You know if it hadn't been for this snake rising up before me and controlling the conversation, and talking only about one tree, and questioning Your word, and suggesting that You were trying to hold out on us, I might not have eaten. Yes, I ate, but the serpent tricked me."

Adam suggested that Eve had some blame (along with God) and Eve pointed to Satan. That's deception, shifting the blame off of your guilt. We point to other people or circumstances, or Satan. But ultimately those excuses blame God who created us and gave us the set of genes that He did. All the while we cover up the real cause, our own choice.

Solomon understood this blame shifting: "a man's own folly ruins his life, yet his heart rages against the LORD" (Proverbs 19:3). That incredible ability to rage against the perfect and righteous Lord while ignoring one's own responsibility shows the despicable horror of sin!

Have you ever blamed God for making you too short, too tall, too slow, too poor, the wrong race, the wrong country, the wrong parents, and so on? The list is endless. The truth is that we are not victims. We make the choice. *Temptation only supplies the choice.* And until we see and admit that clearly, we will not successfully handle our temptations.

II. "The devil made me do it"

> *But each one is tempted when he is drawn away by his own desires and enticed. Then, when desire has conceived, it gives birth to sin; and sin, when it is full-grown, brings forth death. (James 1:14-15).*

If God didn't tempt me, it's got to be the devil. This was Eve's view: "the serpent deceived me, and I ate." "The devil pushed me. He lied to me." "Obviously if Satan hadn't made the temptation so enticing I would not have fallen."

The truth in verse 14 is that **our sin begins with us.** It's our *own desires.* The awful fact is that *we execute ourselves.* We push our own detonator. These two verses give the process. Four participles help us picture the steps into the pit: *drawn away* (as if from some safe place), *enticed* (as if with apple and peanut butter in a rat trap), *conceived* (as in to *seize* and take prisoner), and then the word, *full-grown* (as in mature, full strength).

These four words describe the dark side of trials – the possibility that what is designed for good may become bad, in fact may become so bad that it leads to death. Look at the first two participles which describe how we get things started. They show us that the devil didn't make us do it, even though he's actively involved.

A. We are *drawn away* by our own desires. Sin begins with our desires, not someone else's push. Somehow we can be pulled away or drawn out by desires. It's important to note that these aren't bad desires, because we don't sin until verse 15. They are non-sinful desires. That suggests that the New International version ("evil desire"), the New Jerusalem Bible ("wrong desire"), and the New Living Translation ("evil desires") are misleading. These are desires that can result in sin but they are not sinful. Instead they are normal, human, God-given desires.

Every human has been created with a set of desires that keep us functioning and energized. For example, we need to eat, and sleep, and exercise, and love and be loved, and learn, and accomplish something useful. These desires *draw us out.*

Think of our desire to eat. Our hunger sends us on a search looking for food possibilities. That search provides Satan the opportunity to make suggestions as to what to eat, or how much, or where, or with whom we should eat.

Picture thanksgiving. You've just finished a beautiful turkey dinner with all the trimmings. You couldn't eat another crumb. Someone comes into the dining room and announces, "McDonald's has two big Macs for four dollars. Let's go get some." What's your reaction? *You can't be tempted.* Your appetite has been satisfied and there are no hunger desires pulling you out.

Christ could be tempted because temptation attacks normal human desires. God can't be tempted, but God in the flesh became hungry. And Satan was there to direct, "turn these rocks into bread." He knew that Jesus' normal desire for food was drawing Him out to look for ways to satisfy His hunger. And he was determined to lead Him into deception.

B. The enticement is to fulfill our desire the wrong way.
Enticed is a fishing term that means "bait," or "to get baited." Bait is always something that fish *like.* When desire pulls you out, there will always be bait floating by. It may be from Satan. But it could be other people, friends, enemies, TV, videos, music, your own feelings, your habits. Any of these things can allure, entrap you, literally "hook" you into doing something wrong.

Any of our normal human needs can be enticed. Satan enticed Eve with the fruit of a tree, Christ with bread. Have any of you ever been enticed by pornography? or recognition? or relaxation? You have a need; Satan has an answer.

It's important to realize that *enticement is not sin.* Sin doesn't appear until verse 15 – until desire conceives. Someone has said that it's not the first look at a woman that is sin, but the second. David could have turned away the first time he saw Bathsheba. But his choice to look again created the sin. That's where the truth of verse 15 enters. The fact that Eve saw attractive fruit wasn't sin, until she reached out, took it and ate. Remember that Christ was tempted in all points like we are, yet without sin (Hebrews 4:15). Sin becomes created in verse 15 by our own choice.

III. "It's not going to hurt me"

Then, when desire has conceived, it gives birth to sin; and sin, when it is full-grown, brings forth death. Do not be deceived, my beloved brethren (James 1:15-16).

How many times have you said to yourself, "this won't hurt me; it's only a white lie; I'll do this, get it out of my system and be done with it?" That's deception. That's how we rationalize our sin. The two participles in verse 15 explain what really happens. Once we agree to temptation's suggestion, once we bite the bait, once we say "yes" we start a process that is difficult to stop. It's similar to the physical process of conception and pregnancy and birth.

A. Sin begins when we grab the bait. The phrase, "when desire conceives" results in the creation of **sin.** Sin was not there before. Nothing wrong was present – until desire *conceived*. We could have ignored the enticement; we could have chosen something else. But the word *conceive* means "to seize and make it your own," like what a fish does with bait. We create sin when we go after the bait. The bait plus our agreement give birth to sin. *We bring sin into the world.*

The real source of sin is not Satan. **It's giving in to your own personal desires.** It's agreeing with that word of allurement. "Through one man sin entered the world . . ." (Romans 5:12). It doesn't say, "through Satan." Satan tempts us, but that does not *cause* sin. Sin is only created when Satan finds someone willing to accept his solution to their desires, and seizes the bait.

This process of creating sin is total deception, and Satan is the master of it, the "father of lies." His pitch to Eve was, "God is overstating the case; eating the fruit is not going to kill you; in fact you're going to enjoy it because your eyes will be opened, and you'll become like God." The cleverness of Satan's lie is that he can pitch death as something we need, a fulfillment of our hopes, as something light and refreshing. The embezzler tells himself that he's "borrowing" the money and will surely pay it back. The cheating husband assures himself that what his wife doesn't know won't hurt her. The government worker rationalizes that, "everybody's doing it; why shouldn't I?" as he pads his expense account or steals things from his office.

Satan succeeded with Adam and Eve by lying about the effect of their action. He pictured eating the fruit as **becoming like God!** Nothing about the fact that it would ruin billions of their children. Nothing about the fact that it was opening the door for their firstborn son to become the murderer of his brother and a wandering vagabond. "You'll become like God." *He presented an act that led to death as a Bible College education!*

B. Conception leads to a "pregnancy" and a "birth." I'm thinking of the verb, "brings forth death," which contains a certain amount of relentlessness. Once we create sin, we have a new problem; *we can't stop it.* Sin is habit forming, like a pregnancy, which doesn't stop. It only develops more and more. *When it is full-grown* pictures the maternity ward after nine months of pregnancy.

The conception, which took place when we seized the bait, matures and comes to full term. We "bring forth" a birth. And what is it? It's **DEATH!** Sin gives birth to **DEATH.** "Full grown" speaks of when sin becomes a fixed habit, a power that now controls us rather than something we initiate. And the result is not a whole lot different than a woman who carries a child for nine months, goes through twenty hours of labor, and delivers a *dead* baby.

What does James mean by the word *death*? Is he speaking of losing salvation and going to hell? Think of how Adam and Eve died. God promised that "in the day that you eat of it you shall surely die" (Genesis 2:17). But they didn't die immediately. They were still alive, even though their new need of clothes showed that something had seriously changed. And the fact that they hid from God showed that they weren't the same people. *They did die,* not physically, but it is clear that their desire for God's presence died. That was the beginning of the pregnancy.

The same with us. Most of the time our sin doesn't immediately kill us even though it *instantly changes our relationship with God.* We hide from Him like Adam and Eve. And after awhile, continued sin gnaws on our hearts and minds and we die emotionally, relationally, morally, psychologically. Usually our desire to walk with God dies first, and our love for our children and compassion for the insignificant dies long before we die physically.

So what do you mean when you say to yourself that it's not going to hurt you? It will *kill you* and injure people around you that you love. What do you mean *white lie?* Yielding to the enticement is like opening the door for the smiling terrorist to enter, with her bulging trench coat, it's offering her a room in your house right next to the master bedroom, with no thought about anything other than good, because she is smiling, and happy, and kind, and fun to have around.

Our problem is that we can't see the final effect of sin at the beginning. We even think we're getting away with it. We are having our fun and nothing has blown up in our lives. We still go to church and sing the songs and fellowship with the people. And no one knows what's going on in secret places of our lives. We think we're deceiving them, but the joke is on us. Sin is habit forming. You can't do it once and get away from it. It comes back with power. It won't let you rest until you do it again. After awhile you realize that you are fighting a monster that is *taking over your life!*

"Don't be deceived" James says. "You can't keep yielding to your desires and get away with it. It's death." Think of the tragedy in the past couple of years in Bill Cosby's life, or Harvey Weinstein. Their sin has brought death into their lives and reputations, even though it took years to develop. And ultimately, such sin will result in the judgment of God.

IV. "Satan always seems to have the most fun"

Do not be deceived, my beloved brethren. Every good gift and every perfect gift is from above, and comes down from the Father of lights, with whom there is no variation or shadow of turning. Of His own will He brought us forth by the word of truth, that we might be a kind of firstfruits of His creatures (James 1:16-18).

Temptation always presents the most beautiful girls, the most handsome hulks; Satan always seems to be able to get the real party going. And God often seems to only be saying, "NO! NO!" What does He have to offer in that situation? Here's the real truth behind the fake news – *God is the One who intends the best for us. Satan only lies.*

A. Satan has nothing to offer. Everything good is "from above!" In reality *Satan is bankrupt, he's a ZERO in terms of contributions to our lives.* He has nothing to give. In fact, he isn't interested in giving. All he wants to do is distort God's good gifts. **Every good gift, every perfect gift is from above.** *None* are from Satan. He's a *taker* not a *giver.*

What did he give Eve? The tree was God's. The fruit was God's. The garden was God's. The plan to make Adam and Eve rulers over the world was God's. All Satan could do was call God a liar and suggest that He was holding out on Eve. What did he *give* to Eve? Did he have anything to give her? Did she get life? Joy? Peace? Accomplishment? Extra fruit? *No.* She obeyed Satan's suggestion and found out much later that she had not only ruined her relationship with God but that of all of her children.

Didn't he supply *something? No, that's not his nature!* Jesus said, "the thief comes only to steal, and kill, and destroy" (John 10:10). "Only" describes his nature. He will do nothing else. *And anyone who thinks he will do something else is* **deceived!**

Contrast, the amazing "Father of lights, with whom there is no variation or shadow of turning." God is **the Father of lights**. His goodness is like the sun, which cannot be put out or eclipsed or "shadowed out" in any way. There is no way we can be put in a shadow so that we cannot be reached by the radiance of His goodness.

It doesn't matter where you are, it doesn't matter what you have done. You are not too far from God's Grace when you turn to Him with all your heart. God is the Father of lights, and the source of every good and perfect gift.

Did you notice that after Adam and Eve sinned, Satan disappeared? He wasn't walking with them in the cool of the evening. Was he looking for them when they were hiding? Did he stand with them when God found them? He couldn't care less. They were on their own. All he could do was twist God's Word, posing as if he was giving something better. ***The stupidity of the whole process is incredible!***

And yet humans talk as if Satan actually is making a credible offer! We hear questions such as, "why is everything that is fun, either illegal, immoral or fattening?" Think of what that question suggests: that Satan actually has *fun* to offer. Smoking is *fun*, pornography is *fun*, alcohol is *fun*, exploding and telling everyone off in anger is *fun*, an all-night, wide open party time is *fun*. And God is the One who always says "no" "no," and tries to keep us from the fun.

The truth of the matter is that smoking is not fun. It simply signs you up for the lung cancer ward. Pornography is tragic; it destroys marriages and relationships and true love; alcohol is deadly; an all-night, wide open party can leave you with a brutal hangover, a fresh case of herpes or STDs, or worse, AIDS. Fun? The truth of the matter is that God wants you to be *blessed* – to enjoy His kind of fun, the kind that you can look back on ten years later and say, "that was *good*! Let's do that again."

B. God has given us life with all the condiments. God's purpose in the world is *life* and *fruit*! Satan brings deception and death. God "brought us forth by the word of truth" verse 18 says. The phrase *brought us forth* is striking because it's the same word that appeared in verse 15. When sin comes to full term it *brings forth death*. Here the identical word is used with the result of *life!* He brought us forth, He gave us life by the word of truth. And His purpose in every trial we will ever face, is *life*! He wants His children to be *blessed*.

"First fruits" is another striking word. It suggests second fruits, and third fruits. It suggests that we will introduce others to this amazing Grace and amazing life. We were created for fruitfulness!

Don't let anyone convince you that Satan has fun. I once met a woman who was a fortune teller. She said she could actually tell the future because she was possessed by something her grandmother gave her. When she came to Christ she lost her power to tell the future. She knew it was because the Holy Spirit had entered her life and pushed out the demon who was controlling her.

But she said something interesting about her powers. *None of her prophecies were ever good.* They were always accidents, calamities, tragedies. She reasoned that Satan could predict those kinds of things because he could produce them but couldn't predict or bring about anything good.

That's classic Satanic work. He comes only to steal, kill and destroy. Every good gift comes from above. Don't swallow the ridiculous notion that you are missing out on the good life by walking with God.

V. "I can handle this myself"

So then, my beloved brethren, let every man be swift to hear, slow to speak, slow to wrath; for the wrath of man does not produce the righteousness of God (James 1:19-20).

The "so then" points back to verses 17-18. Since every good and perfect gift is from above and God's purposes on earth are only good, and He intends we become a kind of first fruits, we desperately need more information and help. We don't have the innate ability to stand against these cleverly worded rationalizations. We are like lambs in the middle of wolves. Our chances of success are less than we think.

How do we stand against temptation? How do we experience good and perfect gifts? How do we become firstfruits? The key is to get God's Word into our hearts. These verses explain how that happens: (1) become a listener, (2) speak carefully, and (3) control your anger, since your effort, even to the point of wrath doesn't achieve God's righteousness. You can't do it yourself.

Hearing/listening is so critical because "Faith comes by hearing" (Romans 10:17). We were encouraged to listen in 1:5 by asking for wisdom. We will see listening in 1:23-25 when we interact with the mirror until we see change. The truth is that we will never succeed in conquering our temptations until we listen to God's Word. This is why Jesus said so often, "he who has ears to hear, let him hear!" We all have ears. The problem is getting our minds to meditate on what God says rather than what we think.

Speak carefully because *the first person listening is yourself.* And the greatest deception is *to lie to yourself.* Once you do that, everything else is easy. We sin because we rationalize our choices. James will return to this subject in verse 26 where he says, "If anyone among you thinks he is religious, and does not bridle his tongue but deceives his own heart, this one's religion is useless." The problem in life is how we talk to ourselves and deceive our own hearts. **We need to slow down our speech, listen to what we are saying, and realize how often we talk ourselves into sin.** We sin because we *lie* to ourselves. And we listen attentively to our lies.

Control your anger because righteousness does not come from our frustrated efforts. Holiness takes time to develop. It's like growing up. You can't do it in a day. It takes re-writing the old script your heart has used for years to talk you into sin. That takes practice.

The truth of the matter is that temptation is too strong for us to handle. We don't conquer Satan's bait by some three step technique. He is so clever that he can turn any method on its head and use it against us. The issue is not a technique but daily faith of listening to, believing God and responding to His directions.

Jesus gave the example when He was in the wilderness for forty days without food. When Satan threw out the bait, *He had a verse for every temptation.* "Command that these stones become bread," Satan suggested.

Jesus answered, "it is written, 'Man shall not live by bread alone, but by every word that proceeds from the mouth of God,'" a quotation from Deuteronomy 8:3.

Satan tried again: "If You are the Son of God, throw Yourself down. For it is written: 'He shall give His angels charge over you,' and, 'In their hands they shall bear you up, Lest you dash your foot against a stone'" (Matthew 4:6).

Jesus responded with, "It is written again, 'You shall not tempt the LORD your God,'" a quotation from Deuteronomy 6:16.

Satan tried the third time: "All these things I will give You if You will fall down and worship me" (Matthew 4:9). Jesus' answer? "Away with you, Satan! For it is written, 'You shall worship the LORD your God, and Him only you shall serve,'" a quotation from Deuteronomy 6:13, 8:19 and 10:20.

In defeating Satan's suggestions Jesus did not bring down lightning from heaven. He didn't zap Satan with a nuclear-laser weapon or overcome him by His own omnipotent power. *Each temptation was answered with the words of Moses, a man.* He used a book that had been around for fifteen hundred years. There was something so powerful in what Moses wrote that Satan couldn't handle the words!

Have you ever thought about the fact that the power you need to resist temptation and develop holiness in your life, is in the Bible you have in your hands? All of the power necessary to defeat Satan had been fully available to mankind fifteen hundred years before Christ ever came to earth. Any person back then could have quenched Satan's tempting darts by appealing to those same words!

Yet how many Israelites really listened to Moses and used his words? Think of the tragedy of people chosen of God who possessed omnipotent, demon-smashing power in their hands like Christ demonstrated, yet by ignoring what Moses wrote, suffered defeat time and time again as Satan bashed their moral brains in and ruined their lives?

You and I hold in our hands a *sword* so effective that we as humans *can defeat our most powerful enemy in the universe!* Are you standing by resisting with God's sword? Or are you falling? With the possibility of the greatest life anyone could ever have in your grasp, with the possibility of the *blessing of God*, why would you want to miss it by listening to the greatest liar the world has ever known?

We become doers of the Word as we say "*No*" to these lies and do the truth. Here's the truth about the arch terrorist Satan's lies:

1) Don't think that God has anything to do with your temptation. He doesn't do that.

2) Don't think that the devil made you do it. You made the choice to listen and obey one of your own desires.

3) Don't think that it's not going to hurt you. It will kill you – faster than you think.

4) Don't think that Satan has anything good to offer. He is a zero and comes only to steal, kill and destroy.

5) Don't think you can do it by yourself. You need God's Word. You win by listening to it carefully, analyzing how you talk to yourself about Satan's offers, and not letting your frustrations compel you to make the wrong decisions.

Chapter 4

The Challenge of Listening to God's Word
(and the deception that thinks it's irrelevant)

James 1:21-25

This section talks about the third major influence in our lives as Christians, God's Word. James emphasizes that whatever trials and temptations we face, there is always a God-supplied solution, always God-supplied wisdom available in the Bible. The Apostle Paul said:

> No temptation has overtaken you except such as is common to man; but God is faithful, who will not allow you to be tempted beyond what you are able, but with the temptation will also make the way of escape, that you may be able to bear it. (1 Corinthians 10:13)

There *is a way of escape* so that we can bear our trials and temptations – *always*. Often the issue is not getting God to *provide* a way of escape, because He already has. Rather the question is, "will you pick up, read, and obey God's Word?" *That's where His way of escape is described.*

Jesus gave us a perfect example of being a doer of the Word when confronted with Satan's temptation in the wilderness. He met each temptation with *a verse of Scripture* (Luke 4:1-13). He didn't simply quote the verse; He announced it to Satan as *His intention.* He told Satan what He was going to do with Satan's suggestions *in the language of Scripture*. In all three temptations the Father had provided a way of escape through the book of Deuteronomy.

In this section James says, "become a doer of the Word, because the way of escape is *in the Word*." You want to obey it, not just hear it. Understanding the information does not rescue you. Rather it may bring deception. What's involved in becoming *a doer*?

Is it reading the Bible that makes it effective? Yes, maybe. Is it the listening to a good sermon or Bible lesson? Yes, maybe. This passage shows us four essential practices for the Word to take root in our lives.

I. God's Word Benefits Those Who *Need It*

> *Therefore lay aside all filthiness and overflow of wickedness, and receive with meekness the implanted word, which is able to save your souls (James 1:21).*

Most everybody knows they need the Bible. But there are degrees of need, like the need for vitamins, or a medical checkup every year, or the need for flood insurance on your home. This verse says that our need is nothing short of the *salvation of our souls*.

That sounds like James is writing to unbelievers, encouraging them to come to Christ. But in his introduction James addresses "the twelve tribes which are scattered abroad." Unbelievers would not accept persecution and scattering. These are people who have been scattered because of their faith in Christ. James is directing them how to deal with challenges in their lives as believers.

But why would believers need their souls saved? The word, *soul* here is the word, *life*. It's talking about saving your life. Jesus used this same word in inviting His disciples to follow Him to the cross. He said

> If anyone desires to come after Me, let him deny
> himself, and take up his cross, and follow Me. "For
> whoever desires to save his life will lose it, but whoever
> loses his life for My sake will find it. For what profit is it
> to a man if he gains the whole world, and loses his own
> soul? Or what will a man give in exchange for his soul?
> (Matthew 16:25-26).

Four times in these verses Jesus uses this same Greek word for *soul*. Twice it is translated by the word "life" (v. 25) and twice by the word "soul" (v. 26). Jesus is inviting His disciples to follow Him to the cross. In order to do that they need to say "no" to their desires, take up their crosses, and follow Him.

The value of following Jesus to the cross is that they would save their lives. Such a path may have looked like certain death, but the reality was opposite. Life was in obedience. Should they have quit in order to protect themselves from the persecution associated with the cross the disciples would *lose* their lives in the sense of *waste*.

The invitation was not, "follow Me to the cross so that you will go to heaven." That was an issue of coming to Christ by faith. These disciples had already trusted in Christ. The issue now was obedience. Jesus wanted to introduce Himself to them in deeper ways as they went through the persecution associated with the cross. Missing that instruction by going back to fishing would have wasted their lives.

In a similar way James warns disciples not to waste their lives by ignoring and not obeying the Word. Protecting themselves from obedience would waste their lives. Obedience to the Word would save their lives.

From what do believers need to be saved? Verse 15 speaks of *death*. Verse 16 speaks of *deception*. Both describe the result of yielding to temptation, and missing the life of blessing God wants us to have. Verse 25 says, "this man shall be blessed," meaning "the person who becomes a doer of the Word." God wants His children to live in *blessing*. But blessing is only connected with *obedience to the book.*

One of the problems is that believers don't recognize their need of salvation. They treat the Bible casually because they don't realize the danger they face with deception and death. It's a deception somewhat parallel to that of an unbeliever. Unbelievers need to realize their desperate condition before the gospel becomes *good news.*

Up until the words, *lost* and *heading for hell* dawn upon their consciousness, they enthusiastically charge down the broad way to destruction. As long as they think they are doing pretty well, and God is going to judge on the curve, and they've got some good works stored up, the Word of God doesn't mean much.

A parallel occurs for believers. The value of God's Word depends on a recognition of the danger they face. To view oneself as *saved, and sanctified and on the road to heaven, and forever secure no matter what they do,* tends to make the Bible insignificant.

James says to Christian brothers, "you need your soul saved." Most Christians would ask with surprise, "I'm in danger?" The answer is, "yes, you could blow it all like Esau did for a bowl of soup." "You could turn away from the Promised Land like your Fathers did back in Numbers." God's Word benefits Christians who realize their need of salvation from the deadly effects of temptation. Satan seeks to waste our lives by making us obsolete.

For example, several years ago the story of Mr. Postell came out in the *Washington Post.* He stood in front of Judge Thomas Motley at D. C. Superior Court in April 2015, accused of sleeping beside an office building in downtown Washington.

"You have the right to remain silent," a deputy clerk told Postell, according to a transcript of the arraignment. "Anything you say, other than to your attorney, can be used against you."

"I'm a lawyer," Postell replied. Judge Motley ignored the strange assertion. But then the defendant said, "I graduated from Harvard

Law School in 1979." That got the judge's attention because he also graduated from Harvard Law School in 1979.

The judge said, "Mr. Postell, so did I, in fact, I remember you." This homeless man, who totes his belongings in white plastic bags, haunts the intersection of Seventeenth and I streets, and sometimes sleeps at a church, studied law alongside DC Superior Court Judge Thomas Motley and United States Chief Justice John G. Roberts Jr.

Alfred Postell was one of the top students, always wore a suit and bow tie, was given the Outstanding Alumni Achievement Award by Strayer college. After graduation, he took a job at what was then known as Shaw Pittman Potts & Trowbridge, a respected law firm. He lived on the top floor of the Presidential Towers and enjoyed the rich life.

But for the past thirty years he's been a ghost. The only mark he has made on the public record has been in the form of criminal charges – theft in 1989 in Ocean City – misdemeanor charges in the District in the 1990s. Here's what Postell says: "you become obsolete." You get beyond "your useful life. I was beyond my useful life."[7]

That is Satan's goal – to make us *obsolete,* beyond our usefulness. He wants believers to live in neutral, never having memorized a verse of Scripture, never having the joy of presenting the gospel to an unbelieving friend, never having sacrificed to love an enemy.

Apart from wisdom from this book we tend to blow our opportunities in the Christian life. I attended the funeral recently of one of my Public Speaking students who was an outstanding preacher and teacher already as he took an introductory course from me. I was so excited at that time because he wanted to go back to his home country and be an evangelist. He had all the ability to be a Billy Graham of his country. But he got fascinated by money and the American dream, and never went back. In the process his wife left him, he became mentally unstable and never achieved the potential he possessed. What a waste! He blew his opportunity. That's what bothers James. Either we get involved in obeying God's Word, or **we lose our souls.**

II. God's Word Benefits Those Who *Want Out of Sin*

Therefore lay aside all filthiness and overflow of wickedness, and receive with meekness the implanted word, which is able to save your souls (James 1:21).

You can't listen and understand God's Word when you're in sin, or when you want to hold on to your pet sin. You have to first turn from sin. God opens the words of His book to those who confess and forsake their sin. Notice the precise words in this phrase:

A. "Therefore" - this section is the application of verses 2-20. Do you want to successfully deal with trials and temptations in your life? Then you must do what this book instructs. You will only stand against Satan's craftiness the way Jesus did, by quoting God's Word to yourself and him. It's the Word that will shut him down and give you strength. Very little else has that power.

B. "Filthiness" is a metaphor that describes anything that defiles. It's very similar to our word "dirty." It's like trying to see something with dirt in your eyes. No one can tolerate even the smallest speck.

C. "Overflow of wickedness" speaks of the leftovers, the bad attitudes, the things you remember about people that have kept you irritated. Get rid of them by forgiving them.

D. "All" means every last speck. Confess it. Forsake it. Forgive others. Lay it aside.

You say, "Isn't that a little extreme? I won't get anything out of God's Word until every last ounce of sin is scrubbed out? What is so bad about a few minor sins? Doesn't everyone have a couple?"

Not in their eyes! Maybe you can tolerate a little dirt on your face, but not in an eye. You will do whatever you can do to get one tiny speck out. You will drop everything you are doing to free yourself from it.

This book will keep you from sin and sin will keep you from this book. Your Bible study is not going to be very meaningful until you get passionate about eliminating sin. Confess it. Forsake it. Ask people you have sinned against to forgive you. Pay back what you stole.

Have you dealt with your sin today? this week? It's interferring with your understanding of the Word. It's keeping you from God's blessing.

III. God's Word Benefits Those Who *Capture Its Words*

Therefore lay aside all filthiness and overflow of wickedness, and receive with meekness the implanted word, which is able to save your souls (James 1:21).

A. Our job is to *receive* it. The word *receive* sounds a little passive in my judgment. It actually means "to take with the hand, to take hold of, to get." It describes something you intend to grasp, you want to get your hands on it. And it's a *word*. We are getting hold of words. It's like reading a letter from a long lost friend where we stop and think about every word, evaluating what it says about them, and about our relationship.

The word *meekness* is the word *gentleness* – an attitude that doesn't argue or fight God in what He says but accepts it with appreciation. Meekness realizes who He is, and who we are.

I have had people say to me, "I don't get anything out of it. I read the Bible and it's like reading the telephone book." My question is, "how do you read it? How badly do you want to understand what it says?" The word *receive* suggests that you put some effort into getting it.

That's the way Solomon described Bible study in Proverbs:

> My son, if you receive my words, And treasure my commands within you, So that you incline your ear to wisdom, And apply your heart to understanding; Yes, if you cry out for discernment, And lift up your voice for understanding, If you seek her as silver, And search for her as for hidden treasures; Then you will understand the fear of the LORD, And find the knowledge of God. For the LORD gives wisdom; From His mouth come knowledge and understanding. (Proverbs 2:1-5)

Do you see the *then* that begins verse 5. *When?* Solomon said, "when you cry out for discernment, *And* lift up your voice for understanding, If you seek her as silver, And search for her as *for* hidden treasures." **Then.** The question here is, "do you really want to know God, meet Him and talk to Him?" God gives understanding to those who mount a chase after it.

B. The problem is that words can be slippery. James describes the difficulty: *"for he observes himself, goes away, and immediately forgets what kind of man he was. But he who looks into the perfect law of liberty and continues in it, and is not a forgetful hearer but a doer of the work, this one will be blessed in what he does" (James 1:24-25).*

In verse 24 the problem is, "immediately forgets," and in verse 25 the opposite of a doer of the work is, "a forgetful hearer." In other words, our responsibility is to **get it so we won't forget it.** God doesn't get it for us. He doesn't hold it for us. He doesn't grant us special memory. That's our job – to get it in such a way that we don't lose it.

How hard is that? What do you remember from last Sunday's message? That's four, six, maybe seven days ago. How about the previous Sunday? That may be up to fourteen days old. How about three Sundays back? If we take the analogy of planting seeds, it usually takes seed a week or two to germinate. Suppose it takes the Word of God two weeks to germinate. The question is whether we will still have the words in our minds at that time.

The Bible doesn't accomplish what it can accomplish when we forget the words. And the words don't germinate and produce fruit instantly, by the time you shake the preacher's hand, or close the chapter you have read. They take time. Its effect develops over days, maybe weeks, as we remember and review it. As Malcolm Muggeridge said, "Every happening, great and small, is a parable whereby God speaks to us, and the art of life is to get the message."[8]

How can we get God's message? By being intentional. Take notes when you read your Bible, or listen to your pastor or Sunday School teacher. Ask yourself, "what is God saying here?" and write it down. Memorize a verse, keep going over it in your mind and heart. The more you think about it, the more it will make sense and the more you will see its importance. Pray about it. "Lord You want me to grasp and hold fast Your Word. I haven't done that very well. Would You change my heart, and my habits concerning the way I listen, and enable me to hear, and grasp and keep this Book which is my salvation? May I get hold of something that I will remember for eternity!"

IV. God's Word Benefits Those Who *Obey It*

But be doers of the word, and not hearers only, deceiving
yourselves. For if anyone is a hearer of the word and not a
doer, he is like a man observing his natural face in a mirror;
for he observes himself, goes away, and immediately
forgets what kind of man he was. But he who looks into the
perfect law of liberty and continues in it, and is not a
forgetful hearer but a doer of the work, this one will be
blessed in what he does (James 1:22-25).

Four times in these four verses James emphasizes this same concept: "doers of the word" (22); "not a doer" (23); "not a forgetful hearer but a doer of the work" (25); "blessed in what he does" (25), actually, "blessed in his doing." *Blessed!* That's the same word we saw in 1:12, the same word Jesus used in the beatitudes. "Blessed in what he does!" The *blessing* is only connected with the *doing*.

A. Our responsibility is to do what the Word says. A pastor was teaching a group of his people how to study the Bible. He showed how to identify the promises and commands and descriptions of God in Scripture. Finally, he reviewed and asked, "Now, what should we do with the commands?" A little old lady raised her hand and said with rather triumphant tone, "I underline them in blue!"

You can underline all of the Bible's commands in blue and give yourself a beautifully colored Bible, but they won't benefit you until you obey them. The ultimate purpose of Scripture is not fulfilled until *we move in response and obey.* It takes a personal decision to do something about the command. God does not do it for us. He holds us responsible.

"Count it all joy." Have you stopped when hit with a difficult situation and evaluated the tag you put on that situation? What just happened? Was it the *worst* thing? Was it *miserable?* Or was it God at work in your life testing your faith and producing patience? Have you obeyed and actually counted it *all joy?* That makes you *a doer.*

B. *Hearers only* leads to deception. Again James repeats: "not hearers only" (22); "a hearer and not a doer" (23); "he observes himself, goes away, and immediately forgets" (24); "not a forgetful hearer" (25). Learning God's Word without practicing is not learning. The only way to make sure we understand any verse accurately is to obey it. Anything else will be deceptive (22).

How does deception set in? Verse 24 says we "forget." It's like a man who studies himself in a mirror but doesn't change. "Goes away" suggests that he's busy, has a schedule, and his urgency causes him to ignore what he saw in the mirror. He got a glance but didn't have time to work on it. Think of how silly he will look as he says "good morning" in his disheveled state to everyone in his office.

Jesus described the non-responsive listener with these words: "those by the wayside are the ones who hear; then the devil comes and takes away the word out of their hearts, lest they should believe and be saved" (Luke 8:12).

Jesus says that the devil is always around when the Word of God is sown. If someone doesn't do anything about what they hear, Satan will try to steal it. If the listener is an unbeliever, Satan wants to prevent his coming to Christ. If he is a believer, Satan wants to prevent his growth in Christ. We either capture God's words or Satan steals them.

The instructions to Joshua went like this: "This Book of the Law shall not depart from your mouth, but you shall meditate in it day and night, *that you may observe to do according to all that is written in it.* For then you will make your way prosperous, and then you will have good success" (Joshua 1:8). Success is only promised to those who "observe to do according to all that is written in it."

C. Becoming a "doer of the work" takes time. Obedience often doesn't work at the initial attempt. And verse 25 suggests that there may be a delay: "but he who *looks* into the perfect law of liberty and *continues in it . . .*"

The need for extra time actually appears twice in this verse, in the word "looks," and in the phrase "continues in it." The word, *looks* is defined as, "to stoop down to get a better view." It means to "really look into it." The same word is used in 1 Peter 1:12 of angels who desire to stoop down and look at the amazing Grace God has given to humans. "Continues in it" pictures a person lingering at the mirror.

Do you get up in the morning, go to the mirror and say, "all right, I have to put in my two minutes at the mirror? And then I'm on my way." Do you ever say that with the mirror of the Word?

Think of your experience this morning with the mirror. My guess is that when you first glanced at the mirror it said, "ugh, change." What did you do? Smash the mirror? Say, "you always give me bad reports?" Get discouraged and say, "I can never satisfy this mirror?" Look for another mirror? No, you received the mirror's message as true and accurate even though it said negative things about you.

We don't argue with a mirror. We don't demand a second opinion. We receive its message with meekness. And then we stay there until we have the problem fixed, by shaving it or painting it or spraying it or combing or brushing it away.

That's the point of, "but he who looks into the perfect law of liberty and continues in it." Blessing arrives in our lives as **we stay at the mirror until we see change.**

You went to the mirror this morning because you wanted to see *change.* Do you go to God's Word to see change? To stoop and study? Did you stay there as long as you stayed working on your face this morning? Perhaps if we spent as much time in front of the mirror of the Word as we spend in front of the mirror of the bathroom, church would be different, our lives would be different.

How does God's Word take root? How do we become doers like Christ? **(1) God's Word benefits those who *need it*; (2) It only works as we *confess and forsake* our sin; (3) It only benefits those who *grab it* and *hold onto it*; and (4) It benefits those who *obey it*.**

Perhaps you are asking, "how?" How can I get this book into my system so that it is protecting me? I think the best answer is to memorize it so you can meditate on it. Even a verse a day, a verse a week, a verse of month will give you something to meditate on.

"But that takes a lot of time, doesn't it? And I am busy." Let me give you two examples. Example one: my wife's brother retired from more than forty years with the government back in 2013. How should he employ his time as a former Marine and retired government employee? He took a personal challenge to memorize scripture. He normally walked or ran four miles each morning. So he memorized *as he exercised*. Within a year he had memorized Hebrews, and it became the foundation of everything he talked about. Then he memorized Galatians and Romans.

Example two: one of the things my father was known for was that he memorized much of the New Testament and large portions of the Old Testament. People asked how he did it because he was a busy man. He was the assistant to the chief inspector of the post office, an elder at Barcroft Bible Church, a trustee at the Washington Bible College, the secretary for the national board of Bible Memory Association. He taught a Sunday School class for forty years. He taught in the evening school at Washington Bible College. He must have spent the rest of his time memorizing, right?

No, here's how he did it. He spent twenty-five to thirty minutes on the bus going to work and twenty-five to thirty minutes coming back. During that time his goal was to memorize five verses each day. Sometimes he did four, sometimes three, but he would memorize them in the morning on the way in and review them in the evening on the way out. On Saturday and Sunday, he reviewed the twenty or twenty-five verses he had memorized that week. The point? He memorized large portions of the Bible *without spending hardly any extra time doing it. It was his bus time!*

You and I can do similar things. It's the determination and planning to get it and obey it that make the difference. And it's the realization that this book is my salvation, that its primary job is to rescue me from my sin and give me holiness, and that I am tasked with developing skill in capturing slippery words, so that I can obey them. That's holiness – in real time.

Chapter 5

The Challenge of Religion
(and the deception that thinks it's good works)

James 1:26-27

This first chapter ends with a rather strange and usually skipped-over transition that contains a couple of unusual parts. One of the things is James' use of the word, *religion*. I always thought that Christianity wasn't a religion as much as a relationship. What does James mean by the word? And what is the difference between useless religion and what he calls, "pure and undefiled?"

Another unusual thing is the list. Why are these three items at the top of James' religion list? We tend to overlook them. How important is the tongue anyway? "Sticks and stones may break my bones, but words will never harm me." Is that statement true? James thinks it's *false*.

And orphans and widows? How many orphans have you thought about recently? What is so important about *visiting* them? And *unspotted* from the world? How can the world spot or stain us when we are in Christ? Aren't there more important things to emphasize to young believers, like prayer and Bible reading and holiness? Why this list? James thinks they are of great importance for those who would be "doers of the Word." Let's look at these three issues individually.

I. We Overlook the Importance of How We Talk to Ourselves

If anyone among you thinks he is religious, and does not bridle his tongue but deceives his own heart, this one's religion is useless. (James 1:26).

A. How we talk to ourselves is part of our religion. The word, religion, is the word, worship. It refers to what we do to please God, how we honor Him because He is worth it. Separating ourselves from every other god is worship. Obeying His commands is worship. But here someone thinks he's religious when he's not. He doesn't bridle his tongue. James defines "tongue" as the instrument that speaks to his "own heart." He's talking about one's inner conversation. He's saying that part of our religion is how we talk to ourselves.

This person has talked himself into believing that God is pleased with his life as a Christian. But he is deceiving himself because his tongue is not under control. It's running wild in his heart and getting him to believe delusions, like thinking that he is doing OK with God.

These two verses introduce us to three ways we deceive ourselves:

1. "my words will never harm me"

2. "widows and orphans don't need my help"

3. "the pleasures of the world are harmless"

James has just asked his listeners to quit being forgetful hearers by becoming doers of the work (1:25). Religion or worship is connected with being a *doer of the work*. Now he specifies what a doer does: he controls *how he talks to himself about obeying God*. An unbridled tongue can talk us out of obedience even as it convinces us that we are genuinely worshiping God.

For James a big issue is *deception*. He lived with Judas. So far he has mentioned it four times (1:6-8, 16, 22). Deception will show up again in 2:1-8 with the usher who thinks he is loving his neighbor as he mistreats the poor. It will show up in 2:14-17 with the man claiming to have faith but without obedience. It will show up in 3:9-10 with those who bless and curse out of the same mouth, and in 3:14 with those who think they can teach others when they have bitter envy and self-seeking in their hearts. All of these are examples of living in delusion, like Judas. At the same time these people can *think they are religious* because an unbridled tongue has completely deceived their hearts.

Judas betrayed his own Lord. That's incredible. But what concerns James is that *Judas betrayed himself by his unbridled tongue*. When he walked out of the office of the Chief Priests that day with thirty pieces of silver in his pocket (Matthew 26:14-15), he probably told himself that he had scored big and made a good amount of money. Little did he know that he had sealed his death. Yes Judas deceived others. But the haunting lesson to be remembered is what he did to himself. He was *completely deceived*. And he probably thought himself to be religious.

B. We become what we talk ourselves into. What we say to others is important, but all along James has been talking about *what we say to ourselves*. For example:

"Count it all joy" (1:2) refers to the way we should talk to ourselves about our difficulties.

"Ask for wisdom" (1:5) refers to the way we find God's solution to our problems.

"Let the brother of humble circumstances glory in his high position" (1:9) instructs us to view our difficulties as promotions, because God Himself declares that we are being elevated.

"Let the rich man glory in his humiliation" (1:10), commands us to be grateful for the way trials help us gain the right perspective on our wealth.

"Let no one say, 'I am being tempted by God'" (1:13), instructs us to be careful not to see ourselves as a victim instead of the perpetrator.

It doesn't matter what the trial looks like, God said, "count it all joy because it will cause you to grow in patience." It doesn't matter how we feel. We need to tell ourselves what God has said. We need to replace our conversation with *His statements*. When you say to yourself, "this trial is not something to be thankful for; it's the worst thing that has ever happened to me," you are *lying to yourself*.

One of our greatest projects as believers in Christ is *our own communication*. We're often better at telling others what their problems are. "Do what I say, not what I do" is the outcome. We get ahead of ourselves by trying to help others fix what we haven't fixed ourselves.

Whatever else you do in life, you have to put a bridle on your tongue. Without a bridle your tongue can become an out-of-control fire. Fire that is only directed by the winds is horrible. It kills people. It burns out what has taken years to build. And the major danger of our tongues begins with their ability to deceive our own hearts. *We lie to ourselves, and we believe our lies!*

II. We Overlook the Importance of Less Privileged People

Pure and undefiled religion before God and the Father is this: to visit orphans and widows in their trouble, and to keep oneself unspotted from the world (James 1:27).

Isn't it a little unusual to place one's response to orphans and widows on this list? We acknowledge that our tongues can get us into trouble, and that harnessing them is a struggle. And we understand how the world system can lure us into trouble with its attractiveness. But how can orphans and widows be a crucial part of "true religion?" Why would one's walk with God depend on visiting orphans?

Remember that James is not talking about the kind of religion that gets us to heaven. James is not saying, that heaven depends on visiting orphans and widows and living a clean life. The only entrance to heaven is by the new birth which comes through faith in Jesus Christ. We come to Him as sinners and ask Him for salvation and forgiveness of sins.

James is talking about religion in the sense of *practice*, the holy life celebration we participate in *because we are saved*. Religion is what we do because of what God has done for us. It's behavior motivated by appreciation of God's grace and faith in His directions for our lives.

Pure and undefiled religion before God and the Father involves participating in the suffering of others, especially insignificant others like orphans and widows. That's exactly what the Father has done. He sent His only begotten Son into the world not only to visit us, but to die for us.

J. A. Motyer says that love for the helpless is not an optional manifestation of the new nature, but part of its essence. If you are born again, the very fact that you have been given new life is because of God's caring love for the desolate and insignificant, like you and me. "Is it not, therefore essentially required of those who profess the new birth that they show their Father's likeness?"[9]

A. God Himself has an unusual interest in orphans, widows and strangers. The Old Testament repeatedly emphasizes our need to help them. Take for example this commandment at Mt. Sinai:

You shall neither mistreat a stranger nor oppress him, for you were strangers in the land of Egypt. You shall not afflict any widow or fatherless child. If you afflict them in any way, *and* they cry at all to Me, I will surely hear their cry; and My wrath will become hot, and I will kill you with the sword; your wives shall be widows, and your children fatherless. (Exodus 22:21-24)

Notice the statement: "if you mistreat any member of these groups, I will see to it that your family becomes like them." That is a powerful caution. God personally watches how we treat strangers, widows and the fatherless.

B. We bless God by blessing them. Moses instructed the Israelites to store a tithe of their produce each year so that at the end of the third year they could put on a big feast for the Levite, the stranger, the fatherless and the widow. The goal of the feast was so these people would be blessed, filled and satisfied. God said, "you bless, fill and satisfy them, and you will bless, fill and satisfy Me, and I will bless everything you do" (Deuteronomy 14:28-29). It's as if God said to Israel, "do you love me?" "I will evaluate your love for Me through the eyes of an orphan or stranger or widow." "If you love Me, *they will know it.*"

Does any stranger, widow or orphan know that you love Jesus by your love for them? We sing, "Oh how I love Jesus," but does an insignificant person know that you love her?

C. True family celebrations will include widows and orphans. Moses also instructed the Israelites to make sure they included insignificant people in their family parties (Deuteronomy 16:10-14). He said that they couldn't celebrate the Feast of Weeks to the Lord or even have a good authentic Jewish ethnic dinner without including servants, or Levites, or strangers, or fatherless or widows.

God was saying in effect, "if you want to *rejoice* before Me, make sure you add variety to your gathering of rejoicers." The implication is that *God joins the celebration in the person of the insignificant individual we choose to include!*

D. God is the God of HOPE. Why this special focus on insignificant people? Because widows, orphans, and aliens are three classes of people with less hope. Orphans, for example, are forced to grow up without one or more parents. As you know, the early formative years are what prepares one for life. And to grow up without parents or without the regular input of parental direction and authority makes adult decisions much more difficult. Some of you have come out of that kind of background and can attest to the additional fears and frustrations that arise. But why should we worry about it? Because paying attention to them is *the essence of ministry.* That's the way Jesus defined His ministry (Luke 4:18-21).

What's it like to grow up in an orphanage? I don't know. I grew up in a good family. But Ruben Gallego was born in 1968 in Moscow. His grandfather was general secretary of the Spanish Communist Party. Very soon after his birth, doctors diagnosed baby Ruben with severe cerebral palsy. Unwilling to deal with his disabled grandson, the grandfather had him placed in a Soviet home for handicapped children. Ruben's mother was told the child had died. Instead he disappeared into the USSR's vast institutional bureaucracy, growing up thinking he had no mother or father, and no relatives.

The surprising thing is that he lived through it, and at about the age of thirty-three, Ruben wrote a book about his experiences, typing the manuscript out on a computer with his left index finger, the only one that worked. The book won the 2003 Russian Booker Prize and has now been translated into English. In short, intensely vivid segments, he tells of overcoming heavy odds that would have destroyed most of us. Here's what he says: he was ranked in the eyes of his teachers and attendants as a *retard,* and *a useless hunk of flesh.* And when you're a *retard,* "everyone looks right past you, they ignore you. You're not a person, you're nothing." He said, "at eight, I understood one very simple idea: I'm alone and nobody needs me." He sums up the horrors of his boyhood in a haunting memorable phrase: "the permanent nothing of hospital life."[10]

"The permanent nothing of hospital life." "Everybody looks right past you, they ignore you." "I'm alone and nobody needs me." Can you imagine growing up in that environment? I mean, children who grow up in good families sometimes feel that way, but to grow up where you receive no other information? Day after day those thoughts are reinforced? If you want to read the book it is entitled, *White on Black.*

Orphans represent people with less hope. And God actually calls Himself *the Father of the Fatherless* in Psalm 68:5, because He is the God of people with less hope. Have you ever spent any money or time on orphans or widows?

Here's the problem: we talk ourselves into relegating them to a *less important category.* Then we *fake interest in them.* That's deception. That's hypocrisy. That's what Judas did:

> Then Mary took a pound of very costly oil of spikenard, anointed the feet of Jesus, and wiped His feet with her hair. And the house was filled with the fragrance of the oil. Then one of His disciples, Judas Iscariot, Simon's son, who would betray Him, said, "Why was this fragrant oil not sold for three hundred denarii and given to the poor?" This he said, not that he cared for the poor, but because he was a thief, and had the money box; and he used to take what was put in it. (John 12:3-6).

Judas was bold enough in his hypocrisy to call Mary out as she was worshiping Jesus. He posed as if he was concerned for the poor.

My guess is that he was passionate enough in his interjection that all the other disciples were convinced he had a heart for the poor. But the reality, which came out only a couple of days later, was that *he had no interest in the poor*. He could argue their case probably with some emotion as genuinely religious, but his heart was deceived.

In fact, Matthew suggests that it was right after this event that Judas bargained to betray Jesus for thirty pieces of silver (26:6-15). After living with Jesus for several years and seeing His compassion for the poor, he thought nothing of it.

We can find people who claim to have trusted Jesus Christ as their Savior but no change has occurred in their compassion for the poor. They are as self centered the day after their supposed salvation as they were the day before. James thinks something is wrong. That's not "pure and undefiled religion before God and the Father."

E. The key is in the word *visit*. The word *visit* is not talking about a ten minute stop at their house or orphanage. The word actually means "to look after, to care for." Christ said, "I was sick, and you visited me" (Matthew 25:36), meaning, "you cared for Me." We care for, *visit* Jesus Christ as we are involved in caring for those that others don't want.

Widows, orphans, strangers are people who need care from others because of their unique challenges in life. Orphans need people to step in as parents and encourage and guide them. Widows need people to step in and support them financially and with guidance and encouragement. Strangers need guidance and help to become a part of their new environment.

How can we *care* for these people? There are many ways:

Pray for them. There are one hundred forty million orphans around the world and who knows how many widows, and the billions of insignificant people. Choose a couple of them and pray for them by name.

Spend time with them. Literally *visit* them. Go to wherever they are staying and spend time with them. Invite them to a meal at your place. Once a woman becomes a widow she is out of place, no matter what her age. We had a widow at our church who was twenty-four years old. But suddenly, without a husband, she didn't fit in with married couples. And she was often not welcomed by singles. A divorced women often has similar challenges. Who is going to make her a part of their group? James says, "someone who is genuinely *religious*."

Invest money in them. Feed them, help them, share your goods with them. What does it cost to help feed a child for a week or month? Pennies! And with the stunning amount of money we have as American believers we can't help them? There's a church outside Baltimore, Maryland, that actually constructed and is presently operating a children's home in Namibia, Africa.[11] For thirty dollars a month anyone can get involved in meeting the basic needs of a child somewhere in the world.

Adopt one. Make the widow, orphan or stranger a part of your family by inviting him or her to meals or family celebrations or other special times. Let her live in your basement until she sorts out her problems; give her a car to drive, help her work through the mountain of paperwork.

You can actually, literally adopt a child, like Angelina Jolie, who adopted a four year old boy from Cambodia and a nine month old daughter from Ethiopia. That would be a testimony.

But before that, you can become a foster parent, or you can choose to "adopt" someone by simply making them a part of your family.

The point is that Jesus Christ, God Himself visited us in our affliction and actually "became poor" that we might become rich (II Corinthians 8:9). Nothing short of compassion for the needy on our part will glorify His marvelous example. And the word *visit* in 1:27 calls for a response from each of us.

III. We Overlook the Danger of the World's Spots

". . . and to keep oneself unspotted from the world" (v. 27).

Unspotted is the key word here. What does it take for the world to *spot* or *stain* us? All it has to do is get it's dialog into our hearts in a way that deceives us. We had five wrong ways to speak to ourselves in verses 13-20. "God made me this way and I can't help it." "The devil made me do it." "It won't hurt me," for example. Those are ways we lie to ourselves, deceive ourselves and get spotted by the world. We become convinced that our desires are the key to life. James explains:

> Where do wars and fights come from among you? Do they not come from your desires for pleasure that war in your members? You lust and do not have. You murder and covet and cannot obtain. You fight and war. Yet you do not have because you do not ask. You ask and do not receive, because you ask amiss, that you may spend it on your pleasures. Adulterers and adulteresses! Do you not know that friendship with the world is enmity with God? Whoever therefore wants to be a friend of the world makes himself an enemy of God. (James 4:1-4)

What is it that produces *wars* and *fights* and *murder* and *coveting*? Verses 1 and 3 tell us that it's our *desires for pleasure*. Spots are *desires that control us*. Desires so strong that we fight and quarrel, and even murder.

The word for *pleasure* in verses 1 and 3 is the word *hedona*, which means "minty smell, sweet smell" and thus what delights. It describes people who live for what smells minty, that looks pleasureful, people who've made the conclusion that pleasure is the greatest thing in life.

Verse 3 speaks of how we pray and plead with God in order to get something that we can spend on our pleasures. We look religious as we plead with God to answer our prayers, but in reality all we want is another pleasure toy.

By way of personal testimony, this writer is well versed in the *hedona* form of living. I was about eleven years old, visiting my cousin on his dad's farm in Wisconsin, when I discovered go-carts with big engines. A go-cart with a fifteen horsepower engine that would go fifty miles an hour down a dirt road introduced me to extreme sports. I loved it and quickly chose that I was going to live that kind of life.

I was twelve and in Clarendon, Virginia when I caught a look in a magazine at a woman who didn't have much on. I took another look with lust, and said, "wow, I want to live here, with her."

I was fourteen when I experienced my first speedboat ride. I came to the conclusion that real life would only be found speeding across the top of the water. That started my boat-building desires, which resulted in the building of two boats.

By the age of fifteen I knew that an important goal in life was to become rich, because only as a millionaire could I enjoy the good life. I was sixteen when I bought my first car. I was now free and independent. At seventeen I concluded that real life would only be lived by following the birds, so I set out to become a pilot, to buy an airplane, to fly.

I developed and nourished all of these *desires* in my life that armed themselves to get what they wanted because I knew that getting those things would positively bring me happiness and life. There was no question in my mind that go-carts would bring me life, and women would bring me life, and money would bring me life, that boats and airplanes would satisfy. So my life was a search for pleasure that combined those desires under the title, *Christian*. After all, I had trusted Christ as my Savior and wanted to live for God. I was going to study His Word and learn how to serve Him.

At the same time I was attracted to pleasure. There were desires in my heart staging attacks on my commitment to serve God. They were trying to take over and get me to give up on the serving God thing and live for pleasure. I was *double minded* as James states in 4:8. I wanted both God and pleasure.

I was deceived. My religion was sort of *hedona-religion*, a kind of wisdom that convinced me that serving God had to include my pleasure. I was spotted by the world system.

I mention this personal history because perhaps some of you may have gone in similar directions, maybe not with the same set of desires, but with desires ruling your life as king. Some of you may have given in totally and had a forest fire of burning in your mind, heart and body. Others may have successfully fought the brush fires of desire. But you know what it's like to be *double-minded*, to be *spotted* by the world, *deceived*. That's the challenge, to "keep oneself unspotted from the world."

That's the ghost of Judas again. He was spotted by the world. Money was his god. Remember his reaction to Mary's worship of Christ: "why was this fragrant oil not sold for three hundred denarii and given to the poor?" The question sounds like he's legitimately concerned for the poor and the wise investment of funds. But the next verse informs us: "not that he cared for the poor, but because he was a thief, and had the money box; and he used to take what was put in it" (John 12:5-6).

Can you imagine Judas stealing disciple money? Jesus' entire ministry was probably run on a shoestring. Can you imagine the disciples trusting Judas enough to vote him treasurer? He must have been a master hypocrite. Why didn't Jesus call out Judas for stealing? Why didn't He say, "yesterday we had one hundred denarii in our treasury; today we only have eighty; what has happened?"

The answers to such questions demonstrate the horror of the deception. Certainly Jesus could have interrupted Judas' slide into treachery, but *God does not make the choices for us*. The Holy Spirit convicts us, the Word of God instructs, disciple friends confront and seek to guide us, but when we deceive ourselves it's deadly and it's our own lives that suffer. That's why James is so concerned for his readers.

What we find in these two verses are three important responsibilities that define our worship of God, our religion, our true holiness. Our inner conversation can be so deceptive. As we go to church and sing good songs and give money and listen to the preacher our inner tongue can convince us that we are indeed OK with God. James says, "don't trust that conclusion if your inner tongue is not bridled, if you aren't investing time and money into insignificant people, and if your heart is spotted by the desire for pleasure.

Do you stop to help those who are insignificant, who have less than you? Those kinds of people cannot make you pay attention to their need. It has to come from the inside, from a God-given compassion.

Are you spotted by the world? By video games? By the internet? By drugs? By anger? By wanting to be a lottery winner? If any of these things is true, maybe your worship of God is vain.

What to do about it? *Confess* and *forsake* your sin. *Ask* God for forgiveness and cleansing, and wisdom to worship Him in spirit and truth, by doing His Word.

Chapter 6

The Challenge of Honoring the Insignificant
(and the deception that supposes God discriminates)

James 2:1-13

We started in chapter 1 with three key areas of life that influence whether we enjoy God's *blessing* – trials (2-12), temptations (13-20), and God's Word (21-25). In the last two verses James gave us three examples of *doing the Word* – by not deceiving ourselves in the way we talk to ourselves (26), by actually visiting (getting involved with) orphans and widows in their distress (27), and by actually guarding ourselves from the world's spots (27).

These six items are essential information that should be taught to every new believer in Jesus Christ. You won't walk with God if you don't learn to handle various trials God's way, no matter how many Sunday School attendance pins you have. You won't walk with God if you continually deceive yourself about temptations. And you won't walk with God if God's Word is not in some way making changes in your life.

I have met believers who live for years without any concept of these essentials. They think the Christian life is in baptism and church attendance and giving. That's absolutely true. But of perhaps greater importance is *how a person talks to him or herself about these things.* What do you say to yourself as you go to church, as you listen to a message from God's Word? Are you talking down the pastor?

Judging the people next to you? Complaining to yourself about the air conditioning?

Remember that none of these things involve *becoming* a Christian. He's not saying, "if you don't bridle your tongue or visit orphans you are not a Christian." Neither is James talking about *remaining* a Christian by bridling the tongue. He's not saying, "if you don't bridle your tongue, you are going to lose your salvation." That's not the issue. The issue is our *religion,* our *worship,* our walk with God in *holiness.* James says, "if you think you are in fellowship with God and your tongue is running uncontrolled in your body and deceiving your heart, your religion may not be real. You may be kidding yourself."

The three examples that ended the last chapter (1:26-27) tell us **what this book is about.** Chapters 2-5 are going to develop and apply (a) how we deceive ourselves in our talk, (b) how we look down on or ignore the insignificant, and (c) how we become spotted by the world. Observe, for example, how all three of these issues appear in 2:1-13: (a) an usher is *talking to himself* about people as he helps them; (b) instead of visiting widows and orphans, he is *mistreating a poorer man*, and (c) the *world's spots* show up in his thinking when he assumes that it's right for him to give special attention to someone who looks rich. The usher illustrates how one can "hold the faith of our Lord Jesus Christ . . . with partiality." It's as simple as discriminating against a poor man in seat selection.

I. Discrimination is Subtle

> My brethren, do not hold the faith of our Lord Jesus Christ,
> the Lord of glory, with partiality. For if there should come
> into your assembly a man with gold rings, in fine apparel,
> and there should also come in a poor man in filthy clothes,
> and you pay attention to the one wearing the fine clothes
> and say to him, "You sit here in a good place," and say to

the poor man, "You stand there," or, "Sit here at my footstool" (James 2:1-3).

We grew up in an unfair world. We probably learned to make distinctions between people by the time we were in the third grade. We even had names for them: the bigger, the smaller, the ones with skinny legs, the smarter, the slower, the ones with a different color skin, or different color hair, like the blonde jokes, the bald jokes, the Polish jokes, and so on. We learned to do it, or perhaps we were marked by others who did it to us.

When we came to Christ we met a God who is **no respecter of persons.** Jesus Christ came to this earth to die on a cross for sinners. Sinners weren't sweet little people with bows in their hair and thankfulness in their hearts. They were ugly, disobedient, hateful people, shaking their little fists in His face, as if He was of no importance. These were the people that others didn't like (other than their own mothers), that lied and stole, that everyone knew were going to hell. Jesus not only loved them, He gave His life for them.

And now we have been placed into the family of God, the body of Christ, where we are all declared "equal:" "For as many of you as were baptized into Christ have put on Christ. There is neither Jew nor Greek, there is neither slave nor free, there is neither male nor female; for you are all one in Christ Jesus" (Galatians 3:27-28).

What does equality mean? If we are going to experience God's blessing, part of the work of faith is in how we relate to other people, how we view and treat one another. The truth is that we can't represent the Lord who died for poor and helpless sinners when we have no compassion for poor and helpless sinners.

In our past life, we had favorites. Certain people were easier to talk to, easier to love, easier to get along with. Some people seemed to promise more. Just their presence was different; maybe they were billionaires, or featured on the cover of *Time* magazine, or appeared on *Shark Tank*, or seemed to have an international influence. As a result, all our lives we've looked up to certain people, and down on others. If you have done that, this passage is aimed at you, and me. *God does not discriminate!* And He wants us to become like Him.

This is one of the early projects for every new believer: "how can I become like, and represent a God who is *impartial* – especially in light of the fact that *I have always been partial*, have always discriminated, have always been some kind of a racist?"

What is a racist? Someone who prefers one race above another, someone who believes a certain group of people is superior to others – like WASPs or the wealthy, or blondes, or athletes. They not only prefer one race or group, but they treat them differently.

Think of *Jonah*. He was a seasoned prophet of God. He loved Israelites. He knew they were God's chosen people. But when God assigned him to go to Nineveh, we discover that he hated Gentiles, especially Ninevites and Assyrians.

The entire book tells the story of a loving God working with a stubborn prophet to get him to see God's compassion even on ugly Ninevites. Jonah didn't understand that God was no respecter of persons, and he didn't want to become like the God he represented.

That's the problem every believer faces: "do not hold the faith of our Lord Jesus Christ, the Lord of glory, with partiality."

A. Discrimination involves looking up at or ignoring people. *Looking up at* in the sense of *special attention* and *looking down on* in the sense of *ignoring*. The concept of special attention appears three times in this section. In verse 1 James uses the word *partiality*. The word means "to be attracted to someone's face." It gives a picture of holding someone's face in your hands and saying, "you are so beautiful, you deserve special treatment."

Perhaps the face is beautiful, or perhaps the face is ugly, but the pocket is full of money. The point is that you convince yourself that you should talk *up* to them, flatter them, and give them special treatment.

Verse 3 says, "you pay attention to the one wearing the fine clothes and say to him." *Pay attention* means "to look upon somebody with admiration." What the man says in verse 3 comes out of his admiration.

The concept appears one more time in verse 9: "but if you show partiality, you commit sin, and are convicted by the law as transgressors." *Partiality* is the same word we saw in verse one. You *hold up a face* to give it special treatment.

This usher was influenced by what looked to him like wealth. When a person arrived at the door of the assembly in shabby clothes, the usher immediately noted *poverty* and did the opposite of holding up his face. He gave him minimal treatment. He said to himself, in effect, "anything will do for this guy; he can stand if he likes, or if he's got to sit, why not the floor."

For this usher, certain people didn't count. Perhaps they were the ones mentioned in 1:27 – the widows and orphans, or others who didn't dress very well. What determined the usher's attitude? Clothes and rings. In his mind, he was the gatekeeper in the church of nice clothes and rings.

Clothes and rings suggested that the person had something the church needed, or the usher wanted. Perhaps the usher felt that his active attention would get him something. So he invited the man to sit. In the early days, chairs were provided for elders and scribes, and perhaps other notables. But most of the people sat on the floor.

Can you remember doing this? Your response to someone was influenced by how beautiful they were, or how much money you knew they had, or how important they were, or how you thought they might help you?

Discrimination or racism was *standard procedure in New Testament times.* Jewish leaders like Pharisees taught it as gospel truth. Remember when Jesus said to them, "Woe to you, scribes and Pharisees, hypocrites! For you devour widows' houses, and for a pretense make long prayers" (Matthew 23:14). What were they doing? Praying long and hard as they mistreated widows, as they took over their houses and possessions: "now Lord would you bless this widow as she gives up her house to pay her temple tax. Meet all of her needs, which we have caused." These false teachers could make discrimination sound religious. They acted like they were glorifying God as they ruined the widow's life.

Add to this the huge gulf between Jewish people and Gentiles. Israel was God's chosen people. Gentiles were often seen as dogs. From this we can see how a Jewish person had almost official permission to mistreat Gentiles. But now, in Christ, the command is, "do not hold the faith of our Lord Jesus Christ, the Lord of glory, with partiality."

B. The Lord of GLORY is absolutely impartial. That's one of the things that is so glorious about our Lord. He shows no partiality, no favoritism. He does not choose to treat one person better than another. We find this quality of God announced in Scripture many times. For example:

"For the LORD your God *is* God of gods and Lord of lords, the great God, mighty and awesome, who shows no partiality nor takes a bribe" (Deuteronomy 10:17).

Then Peter opened *his* mouth and said: "In truth I perceive that God shows no partiality" (Acts 10:34). Peter was probably in shock as he made this statement. An angel had just assured him that God wanted him to help a Gentile family come to Christ. Before that, he probably questioned whether Gentiles could even get saved.

"For there is no partiality with God" (Romans 2:11).

"God shows personal favoritism to no man" (Galatians 2:6).

"knowing that your own Master also is in heaven, and there is no partiality with Him" (Ephesians 6:9).

The truth is that the Lord of Glory gave His life for the sins of the world, everyone, the rich, the poor, the Hitlers, the Mother Teresas. And we are going to represent Him by favoring one above another? *Not if He can help it.* To claim a religion that worships Him who loved the world and gave His life for all, while at the same time separating certain people for special treatment is *a perversion of God's grace.* Christ Who died for all is our example. Don't let anyone tell you that God discriminates.

II. Discrimination Damages Relationships

Have you not shown partiality among yourselves, and become judges with evil thoughts? Listen, my beloved brethren: Has God not chosen the poor of this world to be rich in faith and heirs of the kingdom which He promised to those who love Him? But you have dishonored the poor man. Do not the rich oppress you and drag you into the courts? Do they not blaspheme that noble name by which you are called?" If you really fulfill the royal law according to the Scripture, "You shall love your neighbor as yourself," you are doing well. But if you show partiality, you are committing sin and are convicted by the law as transgressors. For whoever shall keep the whole law, and yet stumble in one point, he is guilty of all. For He who said, "Do not commit adultery," also said, "Do not murder." Now if you do not commit adultery, but you do murder, you have become a transgressor of the law (James 2:4-11).

"Wait a minute," I can hear someone say, "what's so *bad* about this usher's reaction? He didn't hurt the poor person. He only ignored him, just treated him differently. Why make a federal case out of it? You can't pay attention to everyone the same way. Try it with your children. It's impossible. You treat everyone differently. So what's the big issue here? Why make such a big deal out of it?" Is James blowing the issue out of proportion?

Mahatma Gandhi practiced law in South Africa as a young man. He intently studied the Bible and the teachings of Jesus because he was attracted to Christianity. Somewhere in his studies he discovered a small church meeting in his locality and decided to attend a service. He was met at the door by an usher who refused to allow him to enter: "there's no room for kaffirs in this church; get out of here or I'll have my assistants throw you down the steps." He was rejected because he was not white.

As a result he never again considered becoming a Christian even though he said to E. Stanley Jones, a long time missionary to India and personal friend of Gandhi, "oh, I don't reject Christ. I love Christ. It's just that so many of you Christians are so unlike Christ"[12]

E. Stanley Jones later remarked, "Racialism has many sins to bear, but perhaps its worst sin was the obscuring of Christ in an hour when one of the greatest souls born of a woman was making his decision."[13]

"So many of you Christians are so unlike Christ." That's the point James makes in chapter 2. "Who was this Man who died for poor and helpless sinners? And how can we represent Him when we have no compassion for poor and helpless sinners?" Becoming a doer of the Word means *getting rid of discrimination.* "Do not hold the faith of our Lord Jesus Christ, the Lord of glory, with partiality."

This usher was not simply giving a rich man a nicer seat, he was *(1) dividing the church of Jesus Christ,* he was *(2) acting like he was God,* he was *(3) dishonoring the wealthy heirs of the kingdom,* he was *(4) honoring God's enemies,* and he was *(5) making himself a sinner.* This act was more than seat selection; it was Satan invading the church through the usher at the front door! Look at the damage James describes:

A. The usher divided the church – *"have you not shown partiality among yourselves?"* All of a sudden, the church was now composed of "haves" and "have-nots." The usher created two classes of people, the better seat people, and the rest. The dividing line was clothes and rings.

A similar thing happened in Galatians when Peter divided the church. The issue was critical because he was pulling others into his discrimination. What was wrong with what he did? All of a sudden, Gentiles were second class citizens in the new church because *Peter decided to stop eating with them* (2:12). He may have politely recused himself from Gentile potlucks, but he was making a distinction between Jew and Gentile. And Paul said, *Never,* and confronted him face to face (2:14-17) to let him know that what he did was not consistent with the truth of the gospel, because God, in Christ has made us all *one.*

B. The usher made himself a judge. *"have you not shown partiality among yourselves, and become judges with evil thoughts?"* He was setting himself up as the one who determined which people were needed in the church. He thought he could judge who would benefit the church and who had nothing to contribute. Maybe he thought he had the gift of prophecy, or could discern motives.

He actually took the place of God. He assumed a position he knew very little about, making a conclusion based on understanding one percent of someone's life while ignoring the ninety nine percent he knew nothing about. What did he know about the rich man's thoughts and motives?

Even more serious, *he became a judge of God!* He made himself a Monday morning, or a Sunday morning quarterback by looking over God's shoulder and thanking Him for sending in the rich man. At the same time he questioned God's wisdom in sending the poor person. In effect, he said, "don't fill our church with these lower class people."

The usher stereotyped people on the basis of insignificant things, like clothes or rings. It's very common: "all blonds are airheads;" "all bald men are _____;" "all Jewish people are _____." How often do we pry apart the body of Christ with our childish distinctions: "they certainly seem to go through the money a lot faster than we do;" "they eat out too often;" "they don't discipline their children the way we do;" "they're sending their kids to public school." And the church of Jesus Christ starts losing parts.

At the same time, it's important to remember that we *are* judges and that we *have to judge in this life*. When you drive a car you need to judge quickly whether the situation ahead is dangerous enough to apply your brakes. You have to determine whether a used car salesman is taking you for a ride, or the guy who offers to put an asphalt coating on your driveway is putting on anything more than old oil. Many times we're called on to judge wisely, and rapidly. But this is different. We're talking about the value of our own brothers and sisters in the family of God.

C. The usher insulted the wealthy, God's chosen ones. *"Has God not chosen the poor of this world to be rich in faith and heirs of the kingdom which He promised to those who love Him? But you have dishonored the poor man."*

James says, "do you understand who you just relegated to the floor? A *Chosen One!*" That's a special title for a Jewish person because they are the *Chosen of God*. And this shabbily dressed man is a chosen one, an heir of the kingdom. Heirs of the kingdom are very wealthy, because the kingdom is very, very, very wealthy!

At the same time this heir may eke out a meager living, may wear shabby clothes, may be missing certain social skills, may not be able to stand up for himself and argue for his rights, and may be very easy to ignore. But God declares that he is rich in faith because he has learned in his poverty to trust God day after day. He may look poor but in reality he's more wealthy than the other guy. He will one day rule and reign with Jesus Christ. And the usher treated him as a nothing.

Most of us Americans are so wealthy that we don't have to live by faith. We can just buy our way out of difficulties – put it on a credit card. We don't have to pray and ask God for help. R. C. H. Lenski makes this insightful statement: "earthly riches are a handicap as far as true faith is concerned."[14] But here's a man who because of his poverty has to trust God regularly. We should be jealous of his position.

D. The usher honored future persecutors. *"Do not the rich oppress you and drag you into the courts? Do they not blaspheme that noble name by which you are called?" (2:6-7).*

James is talking about the rich in general, not necessarily the very man to which the usher gave a front seat. Back in these times, rich Jews were for the most part Sadducees. The Sadducees were the aristocrats, the wealthy, the politically powerful, the high priests of the day. They were the ones who oppressed the poorer Jewish people. And they were usually the ones who harassed Christians. How ridiculous to honor one who will become your executioner while at the same time injuring a genuine friend.[15]

E. The usher sinned. Verse 8 gives the man's inner dialog: *"If you really fulfill the royal law according to the Scripture, 'You shall love your neighbor as yourself,' you are doing well."*

The usher was assuring himself that he was obeying the command to love his neighbor. His tongue was deceiving his heart. He may have had a guilty thought, "yes, I may be treating the poorer man unevenly." But he rationalized his behavior with something like, "there aren't enough seats to go around, and I don't want this man in a white tuxedo to have to sit on the floor. The poor guy is better prepared to sit on dirt." Doesn't that sound legitimate?

But verses 9-11 say that we can't select which law we are going to obey because *the Law is a unit: "you are committing sin." "You are convicted by the law as transgressors."* Verse 10 adds, *"he is guilty of all,"* and verse 11 adds, *"you have become a transgressor of the law."* Partial obedience in loving the rich does not cover disobedience in not loving the poor. Love cannot be selective.

The man was actually breaking the law he thought he was keeping. People can't pick and choose when facing God's moral law. They cannot excuse their failure to observe one part by emphasizing their outstanding observance of other parts. This isn't bowling where you can say, "but I got nine pins down."

The law is like a plate glass window. How many places do you have to break in the window before you have to buy a new one? Remember the Pharisee praying in Luke 18? He boasted that he fasted twice a week. Have you ever fasted twice a week? That's amazing control. But what if he fasted twice a week and was a thief? Or a pedophile? Or terrorist? Now what? You can't pick and choose your laws. Doing one really well while ignoring others makes you a sinner, not a saint. The usher was in sin! *He sinned as he chose who to seat where!*

By this relatively simple act of choosing a special seat for someone who looked rich, this usher, (1) divided the church into haves and have- nots; (2) made himself a judge of who was valuable and who could be ignored; (3) dishonored the really rich people, the millionaires, the poor; (4) gave special attention to the ones who will probably damage the church, and (5) broke the law. So much for a simple ushering job!

It's all so easy. We do it by people we ignore. These are our brothers and sisters. We will spend eternity together. And we walk by them without even learning their names.

One of my teenage educational experiences was with a little old lady at our home church, a lady we called, *Miss Annie*. She had, as far as I knew, only a third grade education, she couldn't read very well, if at all, she supported herself by babysitting for a quarter an hour, and lived in a little house down the street with her sister.

I can remember (with much embarrassment) as a teenager wondering why she was in our church. She couldn't teach Sunday School, didn't sing in the choir, wasn't on any committee. She didn't make any money and couldn't financially contribute. She was just *there*, for every service, Sunday morning and evening, and Wednesday night prayer.

I also remember that Miss Annie could pray. She could get a hold of the Lord in prayer meeting. After awhile I began looking forward to prayer meeting just to hear Miss Annie pray. And she could sing. Her favorite song was "I Feel Like Traveling On." She couldn't read the hymnbook, but as far as I knew she had all the verses of every song memorized. And she sang with all her heart. She belted it out. You could tell that those words were her testimony.

Our church went through hard times, when the pastor left and for two years the numbers kept going down until we may have had not more than fifty to sixty people. But then God brought another pastor in, and within a couple of years the numbers were over five hundred.

I have often thought of the part Miss Annie probably played in that hard time. She attended faithfully because she couldn't walk to another church. Some of the important people, like teachers or the Sunday School Superintendent, or a couple of elders bailed out to attend church elsewhere. But Miss Annie kept praying as she rocked her babies. And I wonder if someday in eternity we will find out that her prayers were the glue that held the church together in its distress. The big names left. Miss Annie stayed and prayed.

Suppose I, as a teen, was an usher in that church on a Sunday morning when Miss Annie came in. What seat would I have chosen for her? Would I have been like this James 2 usher? It's all so easy to do.

III. Discrimination Calls for God's Judgment

But if you show partiality, you are committing sin and are convicted by the law as transgressors. For whoever shall keep the whole law, and yet stumble in one point, he is guilty of all. For He who said, "Do not commit adultery," also said, "Do not murder." Now if you do not commit adultery, but you do murder, you have become a transgressor of the law. So speak and so do as those who will be judged by the law of liberty. For judgment is without mercy to the one who has shown no mercy. Mercy triumphs over judgment (James 2:9-13).

A. The usher faced *judgment without mercy*. He was "committing sin," and was "convicted by the law as a transgressor." He "stumbled in one point" and "is guilty of all." He will be "judged by the law of liberty." And his judgment will be "without mercy" because he has "shown no mercy." Think about how simple and yet how far-reaching his job was. It almost makes you want to think twice about volunteering to be an usher!

Do you see the threatening word in this passage? "judgment is without mercy." What is that like, judgment without mercy? James doesn't explain.

B. Increased privilege brings increased responsibility. We will be judged by the law of liberty. The law of liberty is a law that says, "love one another the way I have loved you" (John 13:34). How can you love him when you give him the *dumpy* seat?

That question expands: How can you love any poor people when you give them your *leftovers*? Leftover change. Leftover clothes. How can you love your missionaries when you give them *stuff you were going to throw away*?

Have you ever purchased brand new clothes or brand new nice things to give to missionaries? Wouldn't that be a way of honoring them? They are our brothers and sisters; they serve God with our support. And we *love* them, don't we? My mother knew a woman who religiously saved her *used tea bags* for missionaries! Used tea bags might have indicated the degree of her love for them.

God is interested that we represent Him accurately. He is no respecter of persons. That means He goes out of His way to help the needy. *Goes out of His way,* means that He calls Himself the "Father of the fatherless." That means He takes special care of the fatherless, they are on His short list of whom to help. He takes special care of widows. *Goes out of His way* means that it was expensive for Christ to leave heaven's glory to live on earth and die for *sinners.* But the Father so loved the world that He gave up heaven's glory to meet our need. What a picture! And He wants us to bear witness with that same kind of love.

If this passage has convicted you that you have a tendency to discriminate, let me give you three suggestions I have found helpful:

1. It begins with prayer. James 1:5 – "if any of you lack wisdom." We need wisdom to know *how* to help those with less than we have. The non-thinking response says, "throw some money at them and be done with it so we can get on with life." But that may not help.

Think of how difficult the usher's choice was in this passage. Let's say they had ten chairs in the room with one hundred people. Who do you give the chairs to? How do you treat the rich man? What do you say as you offer him a seat on the floor? What do you say to the poor man? This isn't a problem that can be solved by a ten page book entitled, *Ushering for Dummies.* The usher needs *wisdom.* How do you display God's love and lack of partiality in social extremes? James 1:5 is the answer.

2. Expand your circle of friends. Don't be satisfied with the present size of your friend family. Meet and talk to new people; draw them into your circle of friends. Invite people for lunch or dinner. Luke 14:12-14 encourages us to invite people to lunch who *can't invite us back*. Get involved in the lives of those who are less significant. Or as Paul instructs: "Be of the same mind toward one another. Do not set your mind on high things, but associate with the humble" (Romans 12:16).

3. Give your best to people. Think about *what* you give away, and *why* you give it away. You don't need it? It's unusable? You want a tax write-off? Have you ever given away your *best* china? You best clothes? Your best lawn mower? – to missionaries, to the poor – to those who need help? Have you ever given away *what you wanted to keep?*

When surgery is being performed on your child, you don't ask what it costs. You want everything done that can be done. How can we carry that same attitude toward our brothers and sisters in the family of God when they are in surgery? Or when we choose what seat they will sit in?

For years Arthur F. Burns was the chairman of the United States Federal Reserve System. He was economic counselor to numerous presidents from Dwight D. Eisenhower in the 50s to Ronald Reagan in the 80s. When he spoke about economic issues, Washington listened.

Arthur Burns was also Jewish, so when he began attending an informal White House group for prayer and fellowship in the 70s he was accorded special respect. No one in fact knew quite how to involve him in the group. Week after week when different people took turns to end the meeting in prayer, Burns was passed over, partly out of respect for him and partly out of uncertainty.

But one week the group was led by a newcomer who did not know the unusual status Burns occupied. As the meeting ended, he turned to Arthur Burns and asked him to close the time in prayer. Some of the old timers glanced at each other wondering what would happen. Burns reached out, held hands with the others in the circle, and prayed this prayer: "Lord, I pray that you would bring Jews to know Jesus Christ. I pray that you would bring Muslims to know Jesus Christ. Finally, Lord, I pray that you would bring Christians to know Jesus Christ, Amen."[16]

Chapter 7

The Challenge of Obeying God's Commands

(and the deception that settles for talk)

James 2:14-26

This section tells us that the word *believe* doesn't always mean "believe" because it is possible to *believe* and not receive the benefits promised to those who believe. Where do we see this? Well, demons *believe*. In fact they tremble. Yet they are not saved. Why? They believe, don't they?

Doesn't the Bible say, "to the one who does not work, but believes in Him who justifies the ungodly, his faith is credited as righteousness" (Romans 4:5)? Why doesn't that seem to work for demons? If they are really believing, why would God not grant them salvation?

I asked this question in a Bible College course once, "Do demons really believe?" I was surprised that four out of the eighteen people answered, "yes." They do? How come they are not saved? If they really believed they would be saved. The point James is making is that *they don't believe* even though they "believe and tremble." They may say they believe; they may even think they believe, but they *don't!*

Verse 14 introduces the subject: "What use is it, my brethren, if someone says he has faith but he has no works? Can that faith save him?" (NASB). James is referring to the kind of faith that talks.

Someone proclaims he has faith. Does he? Is faith something you announce, or claim? Does everyone who says he has it, have it? Obviously not. Then how do you distinguish between a claim to faith and the real thing?

James asks, "can that faith save him?" The issue is the definition of faith. We know that real faith saves. But is a mental or verbal response to God's Word real faith? James has designed this section to clarify the distinction between real faith and dead faith. Notice his four conclusions (all taken from the NASB):

> 17 "Even so faith, if it has no works, is dead, being by itself."
>
> 20 "But are you willing to recognize, you foolish fellow, that faith without works is useless?"
>
> 24 "You see that a man is justified by works and not by faith alone."
>
> 26 "For just as the body without the spirit is dead, so also faith without works is dead."

Four times James repeats that there is a faith that is not faith, twice he pronounces it DOA. It may look like the real article, even sound like the real thing, but the truth is, it's dead. Verse 14 asks, "what use is it?" because it cannot *save*. In verse 17 it is *dead*, "being by itself." In verse 20 it is "useless." In verse 26 this faith without works is "dead," in the same way the body without the spirit is dead.

The missing item in all four cases is "works." Without the required *works* the faith is dead, meaning *it's not faith*. In verses 15-20 James gives us two examples of *dead faith*, one toward people and one toward God. The faith is dead because of the lack of true response. There are good words, good statements of belief, but the expected response is missing. Then in 21-26 he gives two examples of *real faith*, one toward God and one toward people.

What are the differences between these two kinds of faith?

I. Dead faith lacks *works*

> *What use is it, my brethren, if someone says he has faith but*
> *he has no works? Can that faith save him? If a brother or*
> *sister is without clothing and in need of daily food, and one*
> *of you says to them, 'Go in peace, be warmed and be filled,'*
> *and yet you do not give them what is necessary for their*
> *body, what use is that? Even so faith, if it has no works, is*
> *dead, being by itself. (James 2:14-17, NASB)*

A. Example # 1 – a neighbor responds nicely to needy people, but without faith. Someone in the body of Christ appears, a brother or sister without sufficient clothes and food. How should one respond, especially if it might make the difference between life or death?

The neighbor's response sounds great. *"Go in peace, be warmed and be filled."* That's what Jesus said, "go in peace." The difference is that Jesus made the statement right after He stopped a hemorrhage of blood. He met the woman's need, and then said, "go in peace." This neighbor supplied encouraging words but provided no help. The words *did nothing* – "you do not give them what is necessary" (v. 16). The man may have pronounced his words piously. He may have thought of Matthew 6:25-31 and God's promise to supply all our needs, and then left the supply of their needs to God.

The point is that if he believed they were going to be warmed and filled, he would have contributed. His words proclaimed that he wanted them warmed and filled, but he didn't believe what he was saying – because he didn't respond with food and clothes. Instead he probably wanted them out of his sight. Maybe he didn't want to be bothered with the warming and filling.

James states, "the act of giving (his works) would have given life to his words (his announcement of faith)." Without any response to warm or fill the needy people, the words were empty. Thus the conclusion in verse 17 is, "faith, if it has no works, is dead, being by itself." The announcement of faith *be warmed* is in the same category as, *if someone says he has faith* (v. 14). Giving food and clothes to a brother or sister is an act of faith when it is based on the conclusion, "God wants me to believe that these are my brothers and sisters, and to take care of them, no matter what the cost." Just singing or talking about it without doing anything isn't faith. John Wesley said, "Can that faith 'which is without works' save him? No more than it can profit his neighbour."[17]

John says a similar thing in his first epistle:

> We know love by this, that He laid down His life for us; and we ought to lay down our lives for the brethren. But whoever has the world's goods, and sees his brother in need and closes his heart against him, how does the love of God abide in him? Little children, let us not love with word or with tongue, but in deed and truth. (1 John 3:16-18)

Just like the parable of the Good Samaritan, love that doesn't help a needy person is not love. The Priest and the Levite may have declared their love for all, but the wounded man on the side of the road proved them to be liars. In a similar way, faith that doesn't help a needy person is not faith, even though one may say nice words. It's dead.

B. Example # 2 – demons may get emotional over what they believe, without faith.

But someone may well say, 'You have faith and I have works; show me your faith without the works, and I will show you

my faith by my works.' You believe that God is one. You do
well; the demons also believe, and shudder. But are you
willing to recognize, you foolish fellow, that faith without
works is useless? (James 2:18-20, NASB)

Whatever verse 18 is saying, and it's difficult to interpret, it's clear that someone believes there are two ways of expressing faith – with and without works. He apparently believes that James can show faith without works. He may be making the simple argument that people are different. Some people are good at believing; other people are good at practical application of things. Some show their faith outwardly, some don't.

But James won't allow for two types of faith – one with works and one without. Faith *must include works.* There is no such thing as a "non-works" faith. His example is Satan and the history of demons. It's possible for demons to believe things about God without submitting to Him. Demons suggest the possibility of an *unsaved believer.*

How is it possible to believe and not be saved? Didn't the apostle Paul promise the Philippian jailer, "believe in the Lord Jesus, and you will be saved" (Acts 16:31)? Is James saying that Paul was wrong about the sufficiency of faith alone for salvation because it hasn't worked for demons?

No, he's saying that the word, *believe* can be used with a *weaker* definition to mean nothing more than "I believe you." "You claim that Honda makes a better truck; I believe you." Or people will say, "I believe in God," or "I believe Jesus died on the cross." Such statements match the faith of demons.

Demons demonstrate that faith includes two components, a certain *content* ("God is one"), and a certain *response* ("works"). The person ("you") in verse 19 believes that "God is one," perhaps glorying in the fact that he quotes the Great Shema every morning and evening, "Hear, O Israel; The LORD is our God, the LORD is one." (Deuteronomy 6:4).

And James says, "that's good; you are doing well." That's the start, and that's a proper start. But that verse is followed by a command: "You shall love the LORD your God with all your heart and with all your soul and with all your might." Quoting the first part without obeying the second part is not faith.

The speaker may have thought that stating the Shema was an expression of his faith, but James says, "no, demons can go that far and quote the cognitive part of the Shema."

In fact they can believe it so strongly that it produces an emotional response. They fear, perhaps they weep, and they tremble over what they know and accept about God.

But do they believe? Verse 20 says, *no*: "But are you willing to recognize, you foolish fellow, that faith without works is useless?" Their "faith" is useless, their belief is zero. They don't have faith, they don't believe, even though they may claim or show what looks like faith.

James is arguing here that *believe* can possess at least two different definitions. It can mean, *agree with someone*, or it can mean, *obey someone's command*.

Observe how demons can *believe* without *believing/obeying*:

> When He came to the other side into the country of the Gadarenes, two men who were demon-possessed met Him as they were coming out of the tombs. They were so extremely violent that no one could pass by that way. And they cried out, saying, 'What business do we have with each other, Son of God? Have You come here to torment us before the time?' Now there was a herd of many swine feeding at a distance from them. The demons began to entreat Him, saying, 'If You are going to cast us out, send us into the herd of swine.'" (Matthew 8:28-31)

Consider the demonic responses in this event:

(1) They instantly knew and *believed* that Jesus was the Son of
   God. They did not question their understanding of who
   He was.

(2) They were distressed that He had invaded their territory
   ("what business do we have with each other"). They didn't
   expect His presence that day in their territory.

(3) They knew and *believed* that He was their final judge and
   were fearful (they "cried out") that He had come early to
   judge ("torment") them ("before the time").

(4) They *believed* that He had ability to cast them out of the
   men.

(5) They begged Him to let them enter a herd of pigs. They
   believed that He had to grant them permission to make that
   kind of move!

Does this mean that these demons were saved? No, in spite of
the fact that their doctrinal statement looked better than that of
many church members! They knew and believed that Jesus was the
Son of God, that He was their final judge, and that He was their
authority concerning entering pigs. You would think that such
information would immediately send them to their knees in humility
to plead for forgiveness. But, no, they negotiated rather than
submitting. They didn't fall at His feet or plead for forgiveness. They
did ask for permission to enter the pigs, but they didn't call on His
name for cleansing.

The fact that they believed Jesus to be their final judge scared
them into a panic when they saw Him coming. His presence seemed
to always make them very emotional – "whenever the unclean spirits
saw Him, they would fall down before Him and shout, 'You are the
Son of God'" (Mark 3:11)! That was an impressive response! How

many Israelites in the gospels fell at His feet and shouted when they saw Him?

At the same time this interchange shows us that their *believing* was not *receiving*. All announcements that Jesus was the Son of God were not followed by submission to Him, all negotiating with the Lord was not "calling on the name of the Lord for salvation." And even though demons got emotional over the situation because they knew Who He was, there was no genuine faith because they wouldn't submit or receive Christ as their Savior and Lord.

Thus demons show a *faith* that looks like the person in verse 14. They talk about it and get emotional. But to get them to obey and call upon the name of the Lord for forgiveness, which would give them life, is not part of their doctrinal statement.

The faith we find in the Bible speaks of a *response* to God's command. "Whosoever shall call upon the name of the Lord shall be saved" (Romans 10:13). Faith *calls*. Demons might say, "I believe that whoever calls on the name of the Lord will be saved." That may sound like an expression of faith, but the command is to *call*.

Obedience is where demons draw the line. "Sure we believe God. But calling on the name of Christ? That means submitting to him, and no self-respecting demon would ever get caught doing that." They're not going to listen and obey even though they know He is the Son of God because they really believe in themselves. They really believe that they can win the battle and take down God Himself. And even though they know quite a bit about Him and believe that He is there and is the final judge, and tremble over it, their actions show that the real focus of their faith is themselves.

Demons make it clear that there is a type of faith that knows and seems to believe much, can speak well and get emotional. It may look like the real product because of the fear it expresses. But it's *useless*. It's a purely mental exercise, an intellectual agreement on several points of doctrine. The objector in verse 18 apparently thought that intellectual agreement was a valid form of faith – that faith could be demonstrated without works. James says, *no*.

Faith in God is not just a proposition, or doctrinal statement: "I believe God is one." "I believe in God the Father Almighty," or good statements like that. God's revelation also comes in the form of commands. It's not only that, "God is one" (Deuteronomy 6:4), but that, "You shall love the LORD your God with all your heart and with all your soul and with all your might" (Deuteronomy 6:5). Believing a proposition is different than believing a command. You can't believe a command without obeying it.

Take, for example, the story of Blondin, an amazing tight rope walker, who according to stories, strung a wire across the brink of Niagara Falls and walked across. This was back in the 1880s. Then he repeated the act pushing a wheelbarrow. Then, according to legend, he went up to a young person and asked, "do you believe I could take a person across in this wheelbarrow?" The response was, "oh yes, I believe you could do that." Blondin said, "get in." Apparently there was some hesitancy or rejection from the young person to that command.

Question: "could this young person have shown his or her faith *without getting in?*" James says, "absolutely not." The "I believe you could do that" statement is like the demons. They make many of them: "Jesus is the Son of God;" "He is the final judge;" "He has to give us permission to enter pigs." But do the statements mean that they are interested in obeying Him? Never.

What could our young person at Niagara Falls have said or done to demonstrate genuine faith in Blondin's ability to carry a person across? Nothing, *except get in.* There were hundreds of responses that would have been *false faith*. Without the *work of obedience*, without getting in, any other statement of faith would be dead. No matter what the person said or didn't say, the command was to "get in." Even doing other good works would be dead faith. The person could help others get in, could polish the wheelbarrow, could lead the singing of *praise Blondin* songs. But as verse 20 says, it would all be *useless*.

The command in Deuteronomy 6:5 is, "Love the Lord with all your heart." No matter what demons say or don't say they are just polishing the wheelbarrow – if that.

II. True Faith Includes Works

> Was not Abraham our father justified by works when he offered up Isaac his son on the altar? You see that faith was working with his works, and as a result of the works, faith was perfected; and the Scripture was fulfilled which says, 'AND ABRAHAM BELIEVED GOD, AND IT WAS RECKONED TO HIM AS RIGHTEOUSNESS,' and he was called the friend of God. You see that a man is justified by works and not by faith alone (James 2:21-24, NASB).

Includes is an important word in the title. I could have said, "faith results in works," but I use the word *includes* to fit verse 26 where works are analogous to *spirit*. What happens to a body without the spirit? It's dead; useless, non-functioning. The body is only alive when it contains the spirit. Otherwise it's nothing more than a shell, a pronouncement, "be warmed and filled," or a trembly confession, "God is one." As the spirit energizes the body, so works are an integral part of faith.

How can James say in verse 24, "a man is justified by *works*?" Is that true? Does he really mean that a man is justified *by works*? Or that a man *who is justified, works*? In other words, is he saying that works are an integral part of justification because they are an integral part of faith? Or does he mean that justification is by faith, and afterward justification *produces* works? This is an important issue because James repeats the claim in verses 21, 24 and 25.

That claim seems to be the opposite of Paul's claim: "For if Abraham was justified by works, he has something to boast about, but not before God" (Romans 4:2). Paul states that Abraham was not justified by works; James states that Abraham was justified by works. Are both inspired statements? Is this a contradiction?

Both statements are part of inspired Scripture. Both are true. It would be hard to believe that Paul, writing at least ten years after James (*circa* AD 57 versus AD 44 for James), would contradict him. James wants us to see that works in the form of a *response* is an integral part of justification. Paul wants us to see that justification cannot be *earned* by our works.

James is saying that justification is by faith, just as Paul says. But James wants us to understand the correct definition of faith. Action-less faith, or faith that only talks is not faith. Faith has to include obedience to be genuine. It's parallel to verse 26 where life depends on a body *and spirit*. The spirit is an integral part of the body, and apart from the spirit, everything is a quiet nothing.

It's not that the body can function quite well without the spirit and the spirit appears later (sort of like, "we are saved by faith, but works come later"). *There can be no separation between the two. Faith is not faith without works.* That's the point James argues in this section. He gives us two examples.

A. Abraham's faith included obedience. Isaac was the promised son, the family treasure, the beginning of Messiah's line. He was the son Abraham had waited for, trusting God day after day for twenty-five years. His birth was a miracle, born shortly after Abraham turned one hundred years old, and the delight of an old man's life. And now, God not only wanted to take him, but wanted Abraham to perform the work of sacrificing him! What a strange command. You would think that Abraham would have stopped for awhile and asked for clarification. Maybe a small delay might have given God time to change His mind.

Instead Abraham got up *early the next day* to obey God's command. That's a response of faith! He believed that any command from God was good and right no matter how strange it sounded, no matter how expensive it was. Abraham's response was, "let's obey *now!*"

Verse 22 is a key verse: "You see that faith was working with his works, and as a result of the works, faith was perfected." In other words, what he did was motivated by what he believed. He wasn't doing *good works* as such. He could have had a prayer meeting instead of going to the mountain to offer his son. He could have conducted an evangelistic campaign in Canaan. He wasn't doing what we might consider, "the good works that gave evidence of his faith," he was obeying a difficult command. Abraham believed God enough to obey Him exactly, and immediately.

Who knows how much conflict that command must have brought into his heart? Who knows whether he cried all the way to the mountain? But instead of talking about it, or talking himself out of it, he obeyed, collected what he needed, and left home the next morning, on his way to sacrifice his son.

What did he believe? Verse 21 says, "he offered up Isaac his son on the altar." We know he didn't actually *offer* him because an angel stopped him. It sounds like what James is saying is that it was a finished work in Abraham's mind. Before he left home he had concluded that he was going to obey the command fully.

The writer of Hebrews agrees that Abraham had finished the obedience by the time he started:

> By faith Abraham, when he was tested, offered up Isaac, and he who had received the promises offered up his only begotten son, of whom it was said, 'In Isaac your seed shall be called,' concluding that God was able to raise

him up, even from the dead, from which he also received
him in a figurative sense (Hebrews 11:17-19 NKJ).

The way Abraham viewed the event is in the twice repeated
phrase, "offered up" Isaac. We know that he intended to complete
the job because he had concluded "that God was able to raise him
up, even from the dead." The *work* that involved collecting the
needed materials and traveling to Mr. Moriah and assembling the
altar and getting Isaac up on it was all part of finishing what
Abraham had determined, by faith.

B. Abraham's works were works of obedience. Sometimes we
have difficulty with the word *works* in this section because we are so
conditioned by the notion of *good works*. One common conclusion is,
"when people get saved their lives will change and they will produce
good works." That's absolutely true. Coming to Christ will change
your life and make you different. You can't have God the Holy Spirit
in your life and remain the same. And if you think you have trusted
Christ and there has been no change in your motives and actions,
you ought to ask whether the Holy Spirit has actually entered your
life.

But *that's not what James is talking about here.* James is not saying, "if
you have faith, there will be good works as evidence of your faith."
He never uses the word, *good* in this section (14-26). He's not talking
about some nebulous idea of doing good things after we get saved.
People do good things before they get saved. The word, *good* clouds
the issue.

The definition of *works* that James has in mind comes from the
first chapter. It's an important definition:

> But prove yourselves doers of the word, and not
> merely hearers who delude themselves. For if anyone is a
> hearer of the word and not a doer, he is like a man who

looks at his natural face in a mirror; for once he has
looked at himself and gone away, he has immediately
forgotten what kind of person he was. But one who looks
intently at the perfect law, the law of liberty, and abides by
it, not having become a forgetful hearer but an effectual
doer, this man will be blessed in what he does (James 1:22-
25, NASB).

The contrast is between a *doer* and a *hearer only* (or a *merely hearer* or
forgetful hearer). There are hearers of the Word *that aren't doers*. What
does a *doer* do? Verse 25 describes the activity: she or he stays in the
Word like we stay in front of a mirror in the morning. How long do
we stand before a mirror? *Until we see an improvement.* How long does a
doer stand in front of the law of liberty? Until s/he becomes an
effectual doer.

That's an important phrase, *effectual doer.* It's actually two nouns in
Greek, *work* and *doer* – a *work doer.* The point is not that this person
has works and no one else does. Everyone is doing something, often
good. The point is that this person is doing *what the Word directs.* He
stays in front of the mirror of the Word until he obeys it. And the
result is *blessing,* "this man will be blessed in what he does."

God's Word is not simply "truth," like two plus two equals four.
It's *moral truth* that must be obeyed. It's not only a matter of
knowledge or an intellectual exercise, or a fact to be accepted, it is
something to which we submit, something by which we live. God's
Word must be *done.* Jesus said, "but he who *does the truth* comes to the
light . . ." (John 3:21). That's the picture James creates with his use of
the word *works.*

The person who looks into God's Word and stays there until he
obeys what God says will be blessed. The person that forgets, even
though he may say and do good things, will not be blessed. James
uses the word *works* 12 times in 2:14-26. Each time he uses it as *work
doer,* obedience to what the Word directs. Faith is *doing what God says.*

So far in this section, James has given us two pictures of what may look like faith but isn't because it lacks the *work doer* quality. Picture one (2:14-17) depicted faith as talking intelligently and persuasively about what God says. Assure the poor people at your front door that God will take care of them and bless them in spite of how it looks and your refusal to help. *That's not faith.*

Picture two (2:18-20) depicted faith as believing facts about God, even to the place of getting emotional. Demons know that Christ is the Holy One; they know He is their judge; they know they have to ask Him for permission, and they tremble with fear. *But that's not faith.*

Abraham gives us picture three (2:21-24) which shows that genuine faith is *obedience to the specific command that God gives.* In Abraham's case, the obedience was probably the hardest thing he ever did. It may have looked to him like it would cost everything. It probably was the last thing he wanted to do. For sure he didn't feel good doing it. But he obeyed exactly, believing that God knew what He was commanding.

That's the kind of faith James is highlighting in his epistle. He started in 1:2-12 with, "count it all joy," "determine to go through your trial the right way," "ask God for wisdom," "ask in faith," and "glory in your status change." Obeying these commands exactly makes one a *work doer.* You say, "this painful accident I am experiencing doesn't look good, but God said He will use it for good." "And I don't like it, but He said I should go through it fully and not try to lessen the trial in any way." "And He promised I would have wisdom if I asked." Do you live that way? That's living by faith. The activity commanded (*i.e.* "count it all joy") *is the response of faith.*

God says, "I'm going to use your present circumstances to cause you to grow, to cause you to develop patience and endurance. Trust Me and thank Me for the situation." Like Abraham, a *work doer* obeys. That's faith. Lack of faith ignores or adjusts the command when faced with unpleasant circumstances. It may respond by saying,

"I'm not going to count it all joy, but I'll thank the Lord that it wasn't worse." That's not "faith at work in your actions" even though it may sound spiritual.

C. Rahab protected her enemy by faith.

In the same way, was not Rahab the harlot also justified by works when she received the messengers and sent them out by another way? For just as the body without the spirit is dead, so also faith without works is dead (James 2:25-26, NASB).

In what way was Rahab an example of obedience? She didn't have God's Word to obey. She wasn't responding to any specific command of God like Abraham was. But she was taking the next logical step one should take when genuinely believing in God. Rahab concluded that if Yahweh was God, and she was going to join Him, her first responsibility was to protect His people.

She was living in Jericho, a walled city of the Canaanites. She read the newspapers and heard the daily reports of the march of a large group of Israelites toward her city. They had been receiving daily reports for months. They heard how God had dried up the Red sea when Israel came out of Egypt forty years earlier, destroying Egypt's military in the process. They had heard about Israel's battle with Sihon, king of the Amorites and Og, king of Bashan two of the most powerful kings east of the Jordan. Og had sixty cities with high walls and gates and bars. And remember, Og had a mega-king sized bed that was thirteen feet long and six feet wide. He was a big man!

The reaction in Jericho was, according to Rahab, "our hearts melted and everyone's courage failed." Except for one, Rahab. She had begun to realize and believe that, "the Lord your God is God in heaven above and on the earth below" (Joshua 2:9-11). And she wanted to follow Him.

That conclusion changed her attitude toward what she had been taught was the enemy. As a result, when two Israelites came to her house being pursued by her countrymen, she acted according to her faith. That action is described in verse 25 where she, "***received*** the messengers and ***sent*** them out another way." She protected and helped them.

Undoubtedly she had been instructed to kill them, or at least expose their presence because they were the despised invaders. But she knew that their God was God in heaven. Her faith in their God changed her attitude toward these men.

Suppose Rahab *believed* Yahweh was God and *didn't protect His people*. Would there be a way for her to be *justified* while she watched her countrymen execute them? Would there have been anything else she could have done or said? Could she have sung one of Israel's songs in praise to Yahweh? No, her salvation was wrapped up in their salvation.

In reality, she committed treason. She lied to her countrymen at the door. She aided and abetted the enemy. That was faith? Yes, her faith involved, as James says, *receiving* and *sending out* the messengers. She helped them escape the search party.

Do you see the point James is making? *Real faith obeys; real faith acts?* The bottom line is that one doesn't believe *until one obeys*. God said to Abraham, "go sacrifice your son." Abraham could have talked about that command; Abraham could have prayed about that command; he could have added that directive to his doctrinal statement. The key is that he trusted God enough to sacrifice his son.

You don't have faith until you respond; until you exert energy to obey. Faith cannot be solely a mental exercise. "Believe on the Lord Jesus Christ" cannot be only an intellectual assent to the fact that Jesus Christ is God, or that Jesus Christ came to earth, or that Jesus Christ died on the cross for our sins. It has to be a personal response to that message, a response that says, "Lord be merciful to me the sinner" (Luke 18:13), a response that "calls" on the name of the Lord

(Romans 10:13), a response that "receives" Christ (John 1:12), that "comes" to Christ the Bread of life (John 6:35). Passive faith is not saving faith. Simply asserting that you have faith is not faith. Faith obeys.

Noah believed God and moved, and spent eighty years building an ark. He wasn't simply building a boat. He was obeying God. He could have talked about it, could have written songs describing the coming of rain, added the immanency of rain to his doctrinal statement – *and died with the rest of the world.*

In a similar way God has given us commands. For example, Ephesians 4:32 commands us to forgive others. Faith forgives. Suppose you don't want to forgive. Guess what? Very few people who have been hurt by others want to forgive. So what do you do when you don't feel like doing it? *Do it* as an act of faith, believing that God knows what He is doing. Isn't that what Abraham did?

I find that one way to forgive is to first tell the offending person what they did to hurt you, explaining all the negative ways it affected you. Then announce to them that you forgive them fully for their action, and you want to restore the friendship. The word, *forgive* actually means "to send it all away." You tell them that you have sent it all away "as far as the east is from the west!" You will find that the very act of forgiving helps to release you from the pain of the situation. It cuts down your emotional stress.

D. Abraham and Rahab demonstrate the difference between effort and earnings. One of the large questions in this section is, "how can faith be *not of works* as described by Paul and at the same time *require works* as described by James?" How can James say that works are an *integral part of faith* while Paul says that works have *nothing to do with faith?*

The difference lies in the contrast between *earnings* and *effort.* Paul says in Romans 4 that salvation cannot be *earned.* James says, "just because salvation cannot be earned doesn't mean that it is *passive;* faith involves obedience."

The key is that *works* can be defined in at least two different ways.

(1) Work is something you *produce* or *accomplish*. This definition equates ´ work with, "that which is produced or accomplished by exertion or toil; produce; also, anything accomplished; act; deed; feat; as, a good night's *work*."[18]

In this definition, *work* is used in the sense of *earnings*. Work is what I *accomplish*, something I do well enough to impress God, so that He *owes* me the blessing. That's the way Paul defined it: "Now to the one who works, his wage is not credited as a favor, but as what is due" (Romans 4:4). He used the word *works* here to mean something earned so that wages are *due*. An unbeliever who *works* in this definition is attempting to make God his debtor. God owes him righteousness or salvation because of all the goodness he has produced.

But salvation is a *gift*, and everyone knows that a gift can never be earned. When you detect that one of your friends is trying to pay you back for your expensive Christmas gift, what do you think? Do you thank them for trying to pay you back? No, you are insulted, because you intended it to be a gift. Grace has to be *disconnected from any attempt to earn it*. It has to be absolutely free. Your response would probably be, "can't they simply accept my gift and say, 'thank you?'" Attempting to earn grace ruins grace.

But there is a second way that *work* is defined:

(2) Work is any kind of *effort*. This definition uses *work* in the physics sense, the mechanical sense, as anything that *takes effort*. Work is the application of a force or movement against a resisting force, as when a mass is given acceleration, or when someone puts out energy.[19]

Thus the word, *work*, is used in at least two different ways: (1) that which I *produce, accomplish, earn*, and (2) that which *moves*. In situation (1), work means "earnings." In situation (2) work means "effort." The word can mean either *personal accomplishment*, or *personal activity*, earnings or effort.

That's a significant difference. **If Paul is saying that salvation cannot be earned (and he is), he may not necessarily be saying that salvation can have no movement or effort to it.** Just because a person *obeys a command* doesn't mean he earns anything. Faith is not passive. It "calls on the name of the Lord" for salvation (Romans 10:13). "Calling" takes effort. But does that effort earn one salvation? Not at all. It is simply the response of faith.

E. The Bible consistently connects faith with *effort*. Think of the great *faith* chapter, Hebrews 11. Almost all the examples of faith involve verbs, which speak of action. For example:

- "By faith Abel *offered* to God a better sacrifice than Cain" (v. 4)

- "By faith Noah . . . *prepared* an ark" (v. 7)

- "By faith Abraham, when he was called, *obeyed* by *going out* to a place which he was to receive for an inheritance; and he *went out*, not knowing where he was going" (v. 8)

- "By faith Abraham, when he was tested, *offered up* Isaac" (v. 17)

- "By faith Isaac *blessed* Jacob and Esau" (v. 20)

- "By faith Moses, when he had grown up, *refused to be called* the son of Pharaoh's daughter" (v. 24)

- "By faith he *left* Egypt" (v. 27)

- "By faith he *kept* the Passover" (v. 28)

- "By faith they *passed through* the Red Sea" (v. 29)

The evidence suggests that implicit in the Bible's definition of faith is a response that includes effort. The good news of His grace normally comes to us with a promise (eternal life) coupled with a specific command. Faith in the promise includes a response to the command.

For example, how do we know that some of the Israelites actually believed in Christ when He was on earth? Because John 1:12 says that they *received* Him. Israel as a nation *didn't receive Him* (1:11), meaning they refused to believe in Him. But some *did believe in Him*, as seen by their reception of Him. They moved in obedience.

When Jesus said, "I am the bread of life. He who comes to me will not hunger, and he who believes in me will never thirst," the word, *come* expects effort. And *come* is parallel to the word, *believe*. Believing is coming to Jesus. The verse cannot be modified to say, "whoever accepts the fact that I am the bread of life will not hunger" (motionless faith). Or even, "whoever accepts that I am God will not hunger." Or even, "whoever accepts that I will give the bread of life to whoever comes will not hunger." Believing is *coming*. **The act, the effort is the expression of the faith.**

Think of John 10:9 where Jesus said, "I am the door; if anyone enters through Me, he will be saved, and will go in and out and find pasture." Isn't this person saved by faith? Yes, but faith is spoken of as "enter [ing] through Me." What one *obeys* explains what one *believes*.

This blend can be seen many times in Scripture. For example, faith is described as praying without losing heart (Luke 18:1-8). Faith is ascribed to the Samaritan leper who came back to glorify God (Luke 17:15-19). Faith is ascribed to the woman who touched Christ's garment (Luke 8:43-48). In contrast, Jesus ascribed *lack of faith* to His disciples who in panic woke Him up in a storm (Luke 8:23-25). That act showed the absence of their faith.

The sad condition of the Pharisees was caused, not by their ignorance, but by *their refusal to respond to Christ:* "You search the

Scriptures because you think that in them you have eternal life; it is these that testify about Me; and you are unwilling to come to Me so that you may have life" (John 5:39-40). Life was available even for Pharisees if they would believe and obey.

Revelation ends with this invitation: "The Spirit and the bride say, 'Come.' And let the one who hears say, 'Come.' And let the one who is thirsty come; let the one who wishes take the water of life without cost" (Revelation 22:17). The command to *come* is a command to *believe*.

Thus we see in this section how *James has helped us define faith.* The word *believe* does not always mean the same thing. Demons believe. Some claim that they have faith (v. 14). The distinguishing factor is always "works," meaning "obedience." One can claim faith, one can announce faith, but genuine faith obeys.

Chapter 8

The Challenge of Bridling the Tongue

(and the deception that supposes one can serve Christ with unbridled tongue)

James 3:1-12

We are told that one of the strongest muscles in our body (relative to size) is not the leg muscle or one of the back or arm muscles, but the tongue. It's actually a combination of several muscles, that together are amazingly strong and never seem to get tired. But it's true strength is not physical. Can you remember back to the fourth or fifth grade when someone made a statement that still lodges in your heart? You can still hear them say, "chicken," or "four-eyes," or "fat," or "stupid," or "geek?" The tongue is strong enough to put permanent marks in peoples' hearts, like tattoos.

That ability to leave tattoos on hearts is part of the reason James considers the tongue one of the most dangerous weapons known to mankind. It starts fires; it can burn down forests, and families and marriages; it can be controlled by Satan himself, and is less tameable than some of the wildest animals in the world.

And yet people use this weapon every day, often with little understanding of the power they possess or the damage they inflict. What causes James such fear is that an unthinking individual, walking around with a tongue that goes off at unexpected intervals, like an eight year old with an Uzi machine gun, will try to direct a Sunday

School class in a church and blow a few class members away in the name of Jesus. When someone enters a house of worship and randomly kills people it receives worldwide attention. But few notice when the tongue of a leader leaves a church full of people looking like a drive-by shooting has just occurred.

With that possibility in mind, James begins this chapter by commanding, "***go slow on becoming a teacher.***" The command, "let not many of you become teachers," controls the remainder of the chapter. James assumes that his readers are going to say, "Why the caution?" The rest of the chapter gives his answer: *"because as a teacher, you have to use as your major instrument of performance, the most untamable part of your body, the part that is least Christian."* James advises caution: "don't be in a hurry, thinking it's something simple that can be done with little preparation. The truth is that teaching is inherently *dangerous."* James develops this claim in four sections:

I. Few People can Control the Teaching Instrument

> *My brethren, let not many of you become teachers, knowing that we shall receive a stricter judgment. 2 For we all stumble in many things. If anyone does not stumble in word, he is a perfect man, able also to bridle the whole body (James 3:1-2).*

In Jewish culture the opportunity to speak in a synagogue was much more available than speaking in a church today. That's why Jesus could stand up in the synagogue in Luke 4 and speak, even though he was known as the town carpenter. He wasn't given the platform as a rabbi. Even a carpenter could speak.

A similar thing happened with the disciples. They could go into a distant synagogue and speak, even as strangers. And Paul, as a Pharisee, was probably granted the opportunity to speak anywhere.

Coupled with opportunities to speak was a strong emphasis on becoming a rabbi. It was prestigious for a family to have a son training for the rabbinate. There was competition for the privilege of being admitted to Rabbi School because of the status associated with being called, "Rabbi." After all, the root word, *rab* means "great," or "great one." And being a teacher was a position of honor.

But James says, "wait a minute; don't be in too big of a hurry." He mentions three problems that should slow us all down.

A. The consistent testimony in life is that people say and do not do – "we all stumble in many things." We overstate, we exaggerate, we lie, we offend others, we put down others, we mislead, *often.*

Paul described the Jewish nation as a group of people who saw themselves as the official teachers of the ignorant Gentile world. They were confident that they could guide the blind and correct the foolish. But Paul asks,

> You, therefore, who teach another, do you not teach yourself? You who preach that one should not steal, do you steal? You who say that one should not commit adultery, do you commit adultery? You who abhor idols, do you rob temples? You who boast in the Law, through your breaking the Law, do you dishonor God? For the name of God is blasphemed among the Gentiles because of you. (Romans 2:17-23)

He is saying, "you think that you are helping the ignorant and blind Gentile world, but your personal disobedience shows that your instruction is nothing more than blasphemy." Israel was blaspheming the name of God because they could talk far beyond their ability to obey. They could declare their faith in the Great Shema and instruct others what to do, but their faith lacked obedience. They failed at instructing themselves. Christ's strongest condemnations were directed at those who "say and do not" (Matthew 23:3).

Thus teaching has serious prerequisites. How many future teachers were ever warned of this danger? Coupled with our repeated inconsistency is the fact that . . .

B. The standard of judgment is greater for teachers – "knowing that we shall receive a stricter judgment." The grading curve for teachers will be much tighter. God will hold them to a higher standard because their sphere of influence is so much greater. Hurting one person is bad. But hurting a classroom of fifty people by misusing your tongue is far worse.

William Barclay says that in New Testament times rabbis were almost worshiped because they were so high on the influence ladder. Apparently the instruction was that if a house was burning down, the first person you save is the rabbi, then your parents![20]

But James warns that teaching automatically puts one in a different tax bracket of evaluation. Thus it is much more dangerous than we initially believe. Coupled with that is the fact that . . .

C. The tongue is the most difficult part of the body to control. "If anyone does not stumble in word, he is a perfect man, able also to bridle the whole body." In other words, *the last part of the body that a Christian will be able to bridle is the tongue.* There is a very close connection between tongue control and maturity.

King David observed this truth: "Who is the man who desires life and loves length of days that he may see good? Keep your tongue from evil and your lips from speaking deceit" (Psalm 34:12-13, NASB). The person who can bridle the tongue is the one who can bridle the rest of the body. Lack of tongue-control indicates immaturity.

"So," James advises, "you want to make sure you don't get ahead of yourself. Realize that the main instrument teachers must use is *difficult to handle.*"

II. The Tongue is the Major Player in How We Live

> *Indeed, we put bits in horses' mouths that they may obey us, and we turn their whole body. Look also at ships: although they are so large and are driven by fierce winds, they are turned by a very small rudder wherever the pilot desires. Even so the tongue is a little member and boasts great things. See how great a forest a little fire kindles (James 3:3-5).*

A. It's influence can be compared to the bridle on a horse. The comparison in verse 3 is between "bits in horses' mouths" and "we turn their whole body." The issue is how to rule over a horse. Think of the size and strength of a horse. Have you ever been next to or on top of a Clydesdale? Or draft horse? I am told that Clydesdales can weigh more than a Volkswagen, up to twenty four hundred pounds! How large does the bridle have to be to rule over a Clydesdale? A couple of pounds. That means that the entire horse can be directed by something one one-thousandths of its weight!

We can govern the will of an irrational creature with a small bit and bridle. Losing the reins would be like losing control of the horse. In a similar manner, James says, *losing the reins of your tongue is comparable to losing control of your life.*

Solomon agreed when he said: "He who guards his mouth preserves his life, But he who opens wide his lips (meaning, *to let anything go out*) shall have destruction" (Proverbs 13:3).

It's important to understand that James is talking about more than *public* speech. His use of the word, *tongue* includes more than talking to *others*. He's also thinking about how we *talk to ourselves*. In fact, how we talk to ourselves is more important than our public speech.

Where is the evidence that James is thinking about our private dialog?

"count it all joy when you fall into various trials" (1:2). We begin counting trials with joy on the inside, with our inner dialog.

"Ask God for wisdom" (1:5). How does one do that?

"Let the lowly brother glory in his exaltation . . ." (1:9).

"But the rich in his humiliation . . ." (1:10).

"Let no one say when he is tempted, 'I am tempted by God'" (1:13).

How we talk to ourselves is the foundation of what we think, what we believe, what we do, what we say publicly. Then, to make it extra clear, James says in vs 26: If anyone among you thinks he is religious and does not bridle his tongue but *deceives his own heart*, this one's religion is *useless*.

The first deception is to lie to yourself. After that it's easier to lie about what you are doing and to lie to others. Chapter 1 was instructing us to *bridle our tongues when we talk to ourselves*. Bridle it by actually viewing our trials as joy, and not blaming God for our temptations.

Not viewing our trials as joy, or blaming God for our temptations would be parallel to dropping the reins when you're on the back of a wild Clydesdale. You could go anywhere. And the end result is usually first degree damage.

B. It's influence can be compared to the rudder of a ship – This parallel is even stronger because a ship doesn't have reasoning ability or life, as a horse, it cannot be taught obedience, offers dead resistance, it's much larger than a horse, it may be driven by rough winds, yet the whole mass can be turned by "a very small rudder wherever the pilot desires." [21]

It's a picture of how our tongues steer our lives. The conclusion? "Even so the tongue is a little member and boasts great things. See how great a forest a little fire kindles" (v. 5). Our tongues boast great things; *usually to us*. They convince us to dream big. Don't think of the word, *boast* here as an empty boast, that the tongue is simply bragging and talking big. The next sentence shows us the content of the boast; it can take down a great forest. It has the *power* of a fire that boasts against an entire forest. The whole argument here turns upon the reality of the power our tongues possess.

We overlook that power because it seems so small. We're talking about *words*: "sticks and stones may break my bones but words will never harm me." That's completely false, because words can direct one's life to hell. Words can burn down a family, can set a whole church to smoldering. They are the bridle of our lives, the rudder that steers what we do.

Much of what we do is controlled by our tongues. We talk ourselves into doing something and out of doing something else. Then we rationalize, or justify or excuse. We explain to ourselves who we are and what we should be. We constantly carry on a dialog with ourselves.

For example, it was a Black Friday (Thanksgiving of 2003) when I accompanied my daughter and her husband to *Best Buy* to purchase a stereo on sale. When we got there at about 10:45 there were four units left. So I picked up one and found the end of the checkout line which wound halfway around the store. I asked myself whether I wanted this item badly enough to stand in line for the next half hour.

As I was discussing the pros and cons, a teenager cut in front of me, and I thought about saying to him, "did you have trouble finding the end of the line?" "Do you invent the end anywhere you want to?" I didn't, thank goodness, because about five minutes later he put his box on top of other boxes and left, with the girl in front of him who had been in line before me.

I passed through a section of CDs which looked to me like Christian CDs so I read the titles and evaluated whether I wanted to purchase any. They seemed expensive but some offered fifty dollar rebates. I came upon someone handing out candy and decided I didn't need any at that moment. Another employee was handing out free entrees from McDonalds and I thought about how to respond to him.

A woman and her daughter cut in front of me just as I got to the cash registers, so I talked to myself about going up with them to the cash register. I watched as they paid for their DVD and then stood there talking to the cashier. And I waited for probably three minutes as all the cashiers talked to their customers.

Thinking back through that experience, I know that I talked to myself about ten different subjects in the fifteen minutes I was in line. Any one of those subjects could have controlled my actions and led me in a different direction. But I bought my on sale receiver for $139 and now, many years later, we still use it. The point is that much of our life is controlled by the dialog going on in our hearts.

III. An Uncontrolled Tongue is the Source of Major Horrors

And the tongue is a fire, a world of iniquity. The tongue is so set among our members that it defiles the whole body, and sets on fire the course of nature; and it is set on fire by

*hell. For every kind of beast and bird, of reptile and creature
of the sea, is tamed and has been tamed by mankind. But
no man can tame the tongue. It is an unruly evil, full of
deadly poison (James 3:6-8).*

There are six threatening descriptions of the tongue in the first these
sentences:

A. It's a fire. Fire is great, wonderful, necessary, a blessing,
unless it gets out of control. Out of control fire takes on an
independent existence all its own. Verse 5 ended with, "see how
great a forest a little fire kindles." The California fires in recent years
have demonstrated this horror.

According to government statistics, the 2017 California wildfire
season was the most destructive on record. A total of 1,566,344 acres
were burned with more than ten thousand structures damaged or
destroyed with 44 fatalities. This was more destruction than the
previous nine years combined.[22] Most of the fires probably started
with a little flame or perhaps nothing more than a spark.

The tongue can provide a spark. The point is that *our tongues can
start something that becomes independently destructive.* You say something,
and once you let out the words, they take on their own existence and
you can't do anything about it.

It's like a ten-year-old putting a match to one blade of grass and
watching the flame burn down the blade until it crinkles over, and
then up the next blade. It's so small. But before long the woods are
ablaze, and heading for his house where his one year old sister who
he was baby-sitting is asleep. The horror of it all suddenly dawns on
him. As he runs to get buckets of water, he confesses his sin and asks
for forgiveness, he pleads with God to intervene, but *he has started
something that he has no control over.*

You can start a fire that you cannot stop. You can confess it, be
forgiven, but you cannot stop the spreading consequences. Is that

scary? Can you imagine God evaluating my life one day, saying, "Well Schuppe, you started nine thousand one hundred and thirty-three fires in your ministry, damaged more than one hundred and ten churches and forty-four people died because of you?" Our problem is that we don't understand the immense power of our tongues.

B. It can create any and all kinds of evil. It's "a world of iniquity" (v. 6). That means it's "a boundless store, an inexhaustible source of mischief, filth, evil. It contains endless possibilities of sin."[23] The whole dictionary of evil is tongue-based, tongue-encouraged, tongue-accomplished. Jesus said:

> Do you not perceive that whatever enters a man from outside cannot defile him, because it does not enter his heart but his stomach, and is eliminated, *thus* purifying all foods?" And He said, "What comes out of a man, that defiles a man. For from within, out of the heart of men, proceed evil thoughts, adulteries, fornications, murders, thefts, covetousness, wickedness, deceit, lewdness, an evil eye, blasphemy, pride, foolishness. All these evil things come from within and defile a man (Mark 7:18b-23).

And guess how this evil gets out? It begins in the heart with the way we talk to ourselves, the *evil thoughts* we entertain, and then it takes voice and action and produces evil in the world.

C. It can defile any and every part of your body – *"the tongue is so set among our members that it defiles the whole body, and sets on fire the course of nature; and it is set on fire by hell" (James 3:6b).*
Everything in your body gets dirty because of your tongue. It repeatedly defiles the body. How? It plans your activity, it directs your activities, it defends your activities. It sort of supervises what

you are doing. And then after you do it, the tongue justifies it, and excuses it, and defends it, and keeps steering your life.

One small member marshals all the parts of our bodies for wrong. How many times have you re-lived a situation where someone hurt you? You thought about how you would respond, and planned what you would say, and replayed the video over and over until it tightened your muscles, kept you awake at night, and almost turned you into the incredible hulk. All directed by the tongue. It defiles the whole body.

D. It can destroy any event and connection in your life. It "sets on fire the course of nature." The word "course" is the word "wheel." It pictures the circular nature of life which goes round and round. The tongue ignites something at the axle. But the fire doesn't stay localized. As life goes around, centrifugal force pushes the fire down the spokes to the rim, burning into every aspect of life. It turns people bitter, and that bitterness even eats away their physical bodies.

Bitterness destroys relationships. How much slander does it take to set a whole city ablaze? Or a nation? Or start wars? The whole round of existence can burn up by an out-of-control tongue. "An ungodly man digs up evil, And it is on his lips like a burning fire" (Proverbs 16:27).

E. It can even collect its power from hell. "and it is set on fire by hell." Jesus said to Peter, "flesh and blood has not revealed this to you, but My Father who is in heaven" (Matthew 16:17). This was immediately after Peter had confessed that Jesus was the Messiah. Jesus said, "what you have spoken came from heaven."

Only six verses later Jesus said to Peter, "Get behind Me, Satan!" Peter's tongue had ranged from heaven to hell in six verses! How can this happen? We search for words to spit out a response and Satan supplies the choice words we need.

F. It is untamable. *"For every kind of beast and bird, of reptile and creature of the sea, is tamed and has been tamed by mankind. But no man can tame the tongue. It is an unruly evil, full of deadly poison" (James 3:7-8).*

Not only does the tongue do such an enormous amount of damage, but we can't tame it and subdue it to the place where we can say, "now it won't break out like that again." The truth is, "no man can tame the tongue." People often respond to this verse with, "yes, no human can tame the tongue, but the Holy Spirit can. So submit to Him and He will control your tongue."

But is that what James says? Or does he want us to realize that our tongues will *never be tamed?* By the power of the Holy Spirit we can bridle it, but it will never be tamed, so that we can say, "I can now rest, because my wild horse is tamed." The word *unruly* means "unstable," like some caged, wild animal, ever pacing uneasily up and down its den, that cannot be kept down in its place.

Full of deadly poison suggests a rattlesnake or black mamba which can inject a chemical into the tip of a finger that will spread to the whole body. The venom spurted by an angry tongue is often more deadly than any snake poison. One shot inserted into the blood stream of our families or church, one swift strike of our fangs may take the life out of people we love.

The point? "It can be checked, can be disciplined, can be taught to do good and useful things; but it can never be tamed, and must never be trusted."[24]

The process is very simple: we (1) suggest sin to ourselves and others, dreaming about its glory; (2) commit sin, by lying, slander of others (blaspheming the character of another), gossip (talking someone down, instead of going to that person), murmuring, complaining, anger, bitterness, rage, malice, obscenity, foolish talk, coarse joking; and then (3) we excuse or defend our actions – "I was having a bad hair day," or "my heart medicine wasn't working."

This is why Christ said, "there is nothing that enters a man from outside which can defile him; but the things which come out of him, those are the things that defile a man" (Mark 7:18-19). We place such an emphasis on what goes *in.* Does it have enough protein? Right balance of carbohydrates? Vitamins? That's important because you are what you eat. But what about the things that come *out* of the mouth? do they have protein? Right balance of carbs, vitamins? Do they edify? Do they help people grow stronger in Christ? "Whoso keeps his mouth and his tongue keeps his soul from troubles" (Proverbs 21:23).

IV. A Double-Minded Tongue Shows Immaturity

With it we bless our God and Father, and with it we curse men, who have been made in the similitude of God. Out of the same mouth proceed blessing and cursing. My brethren, these things ought not to be so. Does a spring send forth fresh water and bitter from the same opening? Can a fig tree, my brethren, bear olives, or a grapevine bear figs? Thus no spring yields both salt water and fresh (James 3:9-12).

A. What we *are* shows in the contradictions we speak. We excuse our contradictions, but they reveal our character. Out of the same mouth we *bless* God and *curse* man. Maybe not outwardly, but inwardly, we judge and dismiss people with *put down* words. Out of the same mouth we sing praises to God and cut down our brother. We bless God in the Sunday morning service, but when someone irritates us on the way home, we call him by a choice name, a name we save for people we hate.

The word *similitude* is the word, *likeness*, or *image*. The point is that when you curse the one made in the image of God you also curse the prototype, meaning God.[25] The horror of this action is that we actually think it's okay. We can worship God as His children even as we cut down others of His children who are bearing His image!

The apostle John declares: "if someone says, 'I love God,' and hates his brother, he is a liar; for the one who does not love his brother whom he has seen, cannot love God whom he has not seen" (1 John 4:20, NASB).

B. Nature always displays consistency in its fruit. The quality of water gushing from a spring tells us how good the spring is. You taste the water and say, *a good spring*, or *a poor spring*. You don't say, *a good spring* because it has nice flowers around it. Do you expect that a spring will produce fresh water on Sunday and salt water on Monday? *Never*. Why do we get both good and harmful output from our tongues? We may rejoice in the good water coming out on a Sunday morning in church, but what comes out on Monday when we are angry?

If both blessing (fresh water) and cursing (salt water) come out, *only one can be genuine*. Guess which one. When we bless and curse out of the same mouth we reveal the influence of Satan in our hearts. Chances are good that the Sunday morning blessing *isn't real*.

It's the lack of consistency that reveals immaturity. One may bless God with beautiful voice, but when the slander emerges, it reveals that the beautiful voice didn't mean what it said, because James declares, "no spring yields both salt water and fresh."

All of these tongue horrors explain why James started with: ***become a teacher slowly*** (3:1). "Do not rush to instruct others, as if it were something easy to accomplish with little responsibility." The reason is that the teaching instrument is so difficult to control. It's best to start with one disciple, yourself, not twelve, or fifty.

Chapter 9

The Challenge of Bridling the Tongue
(and the deception that thinks it's a quick job)

James 3:13-18

How did James get from a tongue like a fire that burns down a forest in 3:6 to a tongue that produces righteousness in 3:18? What makes the difference? What extinguishes the fire, or prevents its ignition, and instead generates righteousness?

The key is the dialog in our hearts. Change only comes when we start speaking to ourselves with God's wisdom. As long as we listen to the same old dialog, or the way the world talks, or the way things appear on the outside, change will be slight. It doesn't matter how many times we "go forward in church," or have an experience, or see a vision, our lives will not permanently change until our inner dialog changes.

James' thesis in this section is: *it's the inner dialog which produces righteousness in your own life that has a greater chance of producing righteousness in someone else's life.* You talk yourself into obedience and you will learn how to talk others into obedience.

"Talking yourself into obedience" is an unpolished definition of *wisdom*. How does it develop in our hearts?

I. God's wisdom produces good conduct

Knowledge can show up any time, anywhere. It can be spouted by a five year old. Sometimes teens know more than their parents. But knowledge is not wisdom. It is only the start, the preliminary. Wisdom decides how to use knowledge in life's circumstances. It needs a stage like in a theater with people fighting over a can full of gasoline. Then you are given the opportunity to walk up on stage and choose to contribute either a fire extinguisher or lighted match. Knowledge can sit in the audience and tell what will happen with either of those choices. Wisdom has to make the choice, often when it *doesn't want to,* often when nothing in the situation encourages anything more than a lighted match.

A. Wisdom is an action. *"Who is wise and understanding among you? Let him show by good conduct that his works are done in the meekness of wisdom" (James 3:13).*

Knowledge is a noun; it's memory. It's something settled that you can learn. Wisdom is "good conduct" and "works done." It's a decision on how to handle the given options in a situation. It's sort of like *street smarts,* the ability to handle oneself in city street life.

We have a friend who has been in prison for forty years and talks about *prison savvy.* It's a "wisdom" that knows how to act and what to say and do in prison settings to keep from getting killed. Our friend wants to do what's right, but he knows that there are men around him who don't appreciate those who do right. So his prayer often is, "How can I do what's right and make it look *wrong enough* or *neutral enough* so that inmates who hate those who do right will leave me alone?"

Answering that question takes more than knowledge. It takes insight into people and their motives, and how to interact with them. It takes an understanding of what the situation calls for and will allow. You don't learn those things from a book entitled "Prison Savvy for Dummies."

A similar thing happens with God's wisdom. We develop ability to do the best thing as we talk ourselves into obeying God's directions in our trials and temptations. We "count it all joy" when we fall into difficult trials; we "determine to go through the trial fully God's way" and "ask God for wisdom," and "ask in faith," and "glory in our status."

Do you remember those commands from James one? They form the basis of "good conduct" as one becomes a "doer of the Word." Someone has said, "we can be knowledgeable with other men's knowledge, but we cannot be wise with other men's wisdom." Wisdom has to be home grown. It has to be your conversation with God. It's not only knowing how to act in general, or knowing how someone else acted, but knowing what's best in a situation with its unique combination of possibilities and emotions.

The question "Who is wise?" suggests that we reveal wisdom in only one way, by how we act in such specific situations. What we say and do when people don't treat us very well; or perhaps by the way we respond to difficult circumstances; or perhaps in the way we work toward peace in an explosive situation. In other words, wisdom shows up when we face *various trials* God's way (1:2-12).

B. God's wisdom is *good* and *meek*. *"Let him show by good conduct that his works are done in the meekness of wisdom" (v. 13).* Here's what God's wisdom looks like. *Good* is the word "excellent." It describes a choice that fits the situation in a classy way. Jay Adams calls it, "behavior with finesse."

Paul uses this word, *excellent* when he says: "And let our people also learn to maintain good works, to meet urgent needs, that they may not be unfruitful" (Titus 3:14). In other words, excellent works develop from recognizing and meeting specific, urgent needs. This isn't just *doing good things*. It's doing the best thing, the right thing in an emergency.

God's wisdom comes out when His people make decisions that so fit the situation, so help the needy person, so minister to others, that people say, "that was well done."

Verse 13 also contains the word *meekness*, a word speaking of gentleness and humility, a humble attitude of heart, that is much more concerned with the needs of others than its own interests.

James is convinced that if we don't have behavior that is *good* and full of *meekness*, we don't have God's wisdom, no matter how smart we are, no matter how many Bible verses we can quote. And if a person is not making wise choices in his own life, whatever he says to others will not be of much benefit. You can't grow in others what has not been grown in your own heart.

This is why becoming a doer of the Word is so critical. Talking yourself into obedience enables you to bridle your tongue. And when our tongues succeed in teaching us wisdom they are better trained to teach it to others.

II. There's another "wisdom" that produces trash

But if you have bitter envy and self-seeking in your hearts, do not boast and lie against the truth. This wisdom does not descend from above, but is earthly, sensual, demonic. For where envy and self-seeking exist, confusion and every evil thing are there (James 3:14-16).

A. Our inner dialog can automatically pit us against the truth. "But if you have" means, "if you are under the control of, if you are filled with." It looks like James is referring to someone who attempts to speak truth but has bitter envy and self-seeking in his heart.

His two heart attitudes ruin the speech so that he actually argues against the truth he thinks he's teaching. It's the presence of "bitter envy" and "self-seeking" that corrupt the effort.

"Bitter envy" is a form of jealousy toward someone else. "Envy" is the word "zeal." It's an anxiousness to get what you want. It's a form of self-interest, self-centeredness. The word *bitter* puts it into a category that has a bite to it, that adds, "at the expense of other people."

The word "self-seeking" is from the word "hireling," someone who does a job only for pay. It describes a person who serves God *for his own interests,* or *to get paid.* As a result he often promotes things that stir up controversy among people, for his own benefit. These heart attitudes almost automatically turn one into a **taker** rather than a **giver.**

James says, "if you've got these motives in your heart, don't boast or lie against the truth." Don't think you are communicating God's wisdom, because with these attitudes you can't do it honestly. You have to pretend like you're representing the God who *gives every good and perfect gift* when down deep inside you really want to *take things for yourself.*

The bitter envy and self-seeking give your tongue a different purpose, usually *to hide what's really going on.* You may quote Bible verses, but they don't honestly reflect your heart. Instead you're speaking *against* the truth. You are double minded. You are a hypocrite. You're deceiving yourself, like Judas: "why was this fragrant oil not sold for three hundred denarii and given to the poor" (John 12:5)? It probably sounded like it came from a heart of compassion. But it was Satanic.

This is why Paul says, "we have renounced disgraceful, underhanded ways. We refuse to practice cunning or to tamper with God's Word, but by the open statement of the truth, we would commend ourselves to everyone's conscience in the sight of God" (2 Corinthians 4:2 ESV). The words, *renounce* and *refuse* are important words. They suggest that the only method of getting rid of the bad stuff, what's disgraceful, or underhanded, or cunning, or tampering with God's Word, is to *kill it!*

Paul understood that he would never be able to access someone else's conscience with such bad stuff in his heart. So he renounced and refused it in order to reach "everyone's conscience in the sight of God." He wanted his tongue to teach others. But it first had to teach him to "renounce" and "refuse."

B. Our inner dialog can open the door for Satan. *"This wisdom does not descend from above, but is earthly, sensual, demonic" (v. 15).*

What may appear as a form of wisdom is actually *earthly*. It's *pop wisdom*, it's from the world system, the kind we see and hear all around us. It's magazine, TV, video game wisdom. The word *sensual* means that it's what comes from your body, your feelings, your emotions. It's doing-what-you-feel-like-doing wisdom. *Demonic* means satanic. It's the kind of wisdom that demons promote, the stuff that makes them proud. And here it is being taught in the church through someone who thinks he is wise!

The bottom line is that when you have *bitter envy* and *self-seeking* carrying on the conversations of your heart, you may be teaching John 3:16, but what comes out is from the world, the flesh and the devil. Your tongue actually may be lighting fires because it has been "set on fire by hell" (James 3:6). But it even gets worse:

C. Our inner dialog can turn everything bad. *"For where envy and self-seeking exist, confusion and every evil thing are there" (v. 16).*

Notice, "confusion and every evil thing are *there*," no matter what you say, no matter how humbly you say it, no matter how great the speech is. "Confusion" is the word *disorder, chaos*, even *insurrection*. "Evil" is the word, *vile, wicked, bad*. And James adds, "every." The evil, chaotic possibilities are endless.

The horrible possibility is that someone can speak **against** the truth even as they appear to *speak truth*. They may teach the Bible but "confusion and every evil thing are there!" And the teacher may walk out of a Sunday School class with confidence, fully satisfied that he has again boosted his image with another sterling Bible lesson, but the class is left looking like a drive-by shooting. Three students are injured on one side of the class, another student in the back is reeling from the bitter words, and five students over on the other side have received deep cuts. The teacher may be completely unaware of the damage his tongue has caused.

How is this possible? How is it possible to quote God's Word and communicate Satan's message? Because God's wisdom is only communicated by people who have been changed by His Word, changed into actions that are *good*, *excellent*, and done in *meekness* and *humility*. Hypocrites open the door for everything bad.

That may be one reason why Jesus wanted to shut down the "testimonies" of the demons. They knew Who He was: "You are – the Holy One of God!" (Mark 1:24-25). But nothing they said would be of benefit to listeners.

A man once described his Bible training to me this way: "I was taught theology so passionately and so correctly that I learned to hate everyone who disagreed with me." That's sad, to be so educated in spiritual things that it results in hate, envy, self-centeredness, competition, division.

The truth is that you can't hide a bitter heart behind nice words. Heart attitude will always be communicated some way or another. Even as you say, "God loves you and has a wonderful plan for your life, the recipient will hear, "and I don't think much of you;" or "I'm just doing this because I have to."

It's like putting one drop of Ebola sewer water in the two gallons of your lesson. It opens the door for every form of sickness and poison to develop. It doesn't matter how much good water you put in before or after, the one drop from your bitter envy motivation turns it poisonous.

On the other hand someone can be teaching geography, or math and out of his classroom comes righteousness, holiness, and love. What makes the difference, the tongue? No, the heart of the teacher.

Jesus said, "Either make the tree good and its fruit good, or else make the tree bad and its fruit bad; for a tree is known by its fruit. Brood of vipers. How can you, being evil, speak good things? For out of the abundance of the heart the mouth speaks" (Matthew 12:33-34). And remember that He was talking to Pharisees and religious leaders who were teaching Old Testament truths!

Have you ever noticed what goes on in your heart as you prepare to teach, especially the Bible? Here are some of the conversations I've had while preparing Bible lessons:

- "I'm doing this because I have to."

- "I don't have time for this. I am too busy."

- "These kids aren't interested. They're all a bunch of rebels."

- "Wait until they hear today's lesson. It'll knock their socks off!"

- "I'm not accomplishing anything. This class is a waste of my time."

- "All I need to do is get together a couple of stories and keep these people entertained."

- "If I could just get rid of one person in this class, who is making life so difficult for me with his bad attitude."

I'm sure you have experienced similar kinds of conversations. All of these can interfere with the message of God's Word. The danger arises when one of these statements takes over in your heart so that you are preparing to teach God's Word, let's say, *because you have to.*

What do you do when you realize that you have been preparing because you have to? Should you quit because your motive is wrong? No! You deal with that motive and get it out of your system. Realize (a) that God has made you a teacher, (b) Confess your sin and ask God to forgive you and give you a tongue to speak absolute truth, (c) and then pray as the psalmists did: "Set a guard, O Lord, over my mouth; keep watch over the door of my lips" (Psalm 141:3).

What you're praying for is the *bridle* to reign in the tongue that's speaking in your heart.

III. God's Wisdom will result in righteousness

But the wisdom that is from above is first pure, then peaceable, gentle, willing to yield, full of mercy and good fruits, without partiality and without hypocrisy. Now the fruit of righteousness is sown in peace by those who make peace (James 3:17-18).

The picture in verse 18 is of a farmer planting seeds that produce a crop of righteousness. It's the "good conduct" and the "works done in the meekness of wisdom" from verse 13 that people see and hear, and like and want. And righteousness appears in the hearts of others, just like the young teachers in verse 1 desire! How does the process work?

Make peace states the work, resolving problems, quieting emotions, reasoning with unreasonable people, not allowing the doors to close and the gunfire to begin. To do this one has to genuinely *want peace*. That motivation is *purity at work*. Purity says, "it's more fun to create peace than watching a fight, or taking sides."

Making peace takes skill, being able to negotiate, handle out-of-control emotions, calm angry tensions and frustrations, focus people on higher goals. The employment of these skills in God's work plants seeds in the hearts of people that sprout in righteousness.

Wouldn't you like to see that? You talk to someone and righteousness blossoms. You hang out with friends and they want to know more about Jesus. The seeds which grow into righteousness are sown by people who honestly want to make peace, honestly want to help people work things out so that they can get along and work together and build a family.

A. God's wisdom starts only with purity. *"first pure . . ."* Actions that are "done in the meekness of wisdom" are "first pure." That sounds almost like an oxymoron. Wisdom depends on purity while at the same time purity develops through wisdom. How does that work?

The answer is in the definition of *purity*. The word doesn't mean *never make a mistake*. *Pure* means that your sins are forgiven, that your relationships with others are straight, or as straight as you can make them, and that your heart is right with God. It's a word that means "separated" from the sin we used to live in.

It might mean being separated from people that encourage us to sin. It may involve being separated from actions that led us into sin, like getting angry and popping off. It may involve being separated from wrong inner dialog. The process of growing in Christ is a process of being separated from the old life and embracing the new life.

One of the helpful pictures to me is the picture of Old Testament priests. What did the priests do to purify themselves, before they began their service, or before they offered sacrifices, or entered the holy of holies? They washed their hands and feet and took a bath. Four times on the day of atonement in Leviticus 16, the priest is instructed to take a bath.

Why? It was a picture of separation. He washed off the dirt that collected on him even as he served God. A pure person is someone who repeatedly washes his hands and feet by confessing and forsaking his dirt. *Purity depends on repeatedly separating ourselves from all the stuff that attacks us, mentally, morally, emotionally.*

Ten verses later James will say: "Cleanse *your* hands, *you* sinners; and purify *your* hearts, *you* double-minded" (4:8). The cleansing and the purifying go together, and the hands and the hearts fit together. Purifying your heart is like washing dirty hands. It's a matter of confessing your sin (1 John 1:9) and forsaking it and continuing to confess and forsake every time your inner dialog gets hijacked by deceptive words.

The word, *first* is important because it's not talking about a number. James isn't saying, "*purity* is number one and number two is *peaceable*, then number three." Purity is not first numerically, but rather *essentially. God's wisdom only begins with purity. Essentially* means that you won't see the rest of the qualities if the first one is not present. Purity is the root. All other qualities grow out of it. Every other quality of wisdom depends on washing our hands, confessing our sin, separating ourselves from that which taints the inner dialog of our hearts.

B. Out of purity come other attractive qualities. It's sort of like purity is the wake-up call that opens our minds to a constellation of beautiful characteristics. Each of these characteristics develops in the way we talk to ourselves.

PEACEABLE – the sin that so easily enters our lives is the sin of *strife* as in verses 14 and 16, *envy* and *self-seeking*. But the good news is that the Holy Spirit can enable us to repeatedly wash our hands of an inner dialog of competition, a desire to get our own way at all costs. As a result we come to understand that there is another kind of victory, a victory that comes from consensus, from respect, from dialog, rather than from self-centered accomplishment, from servanthood rather than dictatorship (Mark 10:43-44).

GENTLE – This word means "reasonable." It's someone who does not stand on his rights, is not harsh with others. The word describes a listener who will genuinely focus on what others are saying. Where does this come from? It's a fruit that the Holy Spirit grows in us as we wash your hands of pride and self-centeredness (Galatians 5:23). Our society wants us to insist on our rights. God's wisdom reveals that there is something more important than getting our rights.

WILLING TO YIELD – This is a person who doesn't have it all figured out. He doesn't pose as the final judge. He's open to the suggestions of others. He understands the value of group input.

I've learned that God's will is often best understood by a group. People need to get together and talk about what God wants them to do. God reveals His will as people share their convictions and listen to others.

For example, as a pastor I have gone into a leadership meeting with an idea I felt was right. I would announce it and then sometimes be surprised when the leaders didn't agree with me. One time they even thought my decision was a little silly, and wrong! I felt the temptation to get defensive, thinking they were trying to attack my character.

What I needed was to wash my hands of the attitude inside me that said, "you know, I can do what I want to do here, because I'm the pastor," "you know, I'm older than you." It is never easy to yield. And we don't yield, except as we deal with the self-seeking dirt that clings to us. Once I yielded, I realized that they were right.

FULL OF MERCY AND GOOD FRUITS – Mercy is knowing what to overlook. Mercy delays judgment, mercy overlooks certain sins so that grace might be able to enter and forgive them. It's like parents, picking their battles by overlooking the sassiness of their teen in order to help him or her with something more important.

Mercy is that incredible quality of God. The only reason you and I are alive today is because God has overlooked what we have done. We have sinned enough to go to hell instantly. The only reason we aren't burning in hell right now is the mercy of God.

God delays His judgment on our sins, with the desire that we will hear the good news that Jesus Christ has paid for our sins, that we will trust Him as Savior, and be forgiven. There is a short space of time that God has granted to every person, a window of mercy, where judgment is delayed. And God says, "today is the day of salvation."

God's wisdom displays this quality of mercy and good fruits. He develops mercy in us as we wash our hands from our attitudes of playing judge, of keeping talleys, of remembering where we have to pay people back for their transgressions against us. Also remembering how merciful the final Judge has been of us (Matthew 18:32-33).

WITHOUT PARTIALITY – partiality treats people in different ways, often according to what they have to offer us. The usher in James 2 divided the congregants according to how rich they looked, and what promise their clothes or rings offered to the church budget. We divide people by race or religion or size or economic status, or any number of things. There is nothing wrong with saying, "how beautiful," or "how brilliant," or "what an athlete," or, "think of what this person would contribute to our church."

The problem comes when we treat the person with special treatment that we don't likewise supply to the "not so beautiful," or "not so brilliant," or "non athletes." However good our reasons are, the act of making distinctions is wrong: "but if you show partiality, you commit sin, and are convicted by the law as transgressors" (James 2:9).

The way we treat people comes out of our inner dialog. We look up to them and give them extra credit. Or we judge them and look down on them. It's a matter of washing our hands of our deceptive talk.

WITHOUT HYPOCRISY – Hypocrisy is *acting as if you are someone you are not*. This involves playing a part, wearing a mask, so that people don't meet *the real you*; acting religious when you have a heart of bitter jealousy and envy; speaking to please others when your heart is really saying something else.

Thomas Jefferson said, "honesty is the first chapter in the book of wisdom."[26] How does God develop honesty in us? As we wash our hands of every attempt to deceive, as we admit our hypocritical hearts, our lying tongues, our misleading implications, God works in our hearts.

James is asking the question, "do you want God's wisdom? Do you want to be a teacher God uses?" His answer is, "get serious about repeatedly washing your hands, talking absolute truth to yourself, and controlling your desires."

This chapter ends with, "behold I show you a better way." It began with those who passionately wanted to become teachers. James began by cautioning, "remember that you have to use as your major instrument of performance, the most un-tamable part of your body, your tongue."

Now he closes with, *"before you jump into teaching, learn to plant seeds that will bear the fruit of righteousness; learn to make peace."* A good way to pray is to ask God for the wisdom and ability to bridle your tongue, not only outwardly, but inwardly. That's the way the Psalmist prayed: "Let the words of my mouth and the meditation of my heart Be acceptable in Your sight, O LORD, my strength and my Redeemer" (Psalm 19:14).

Chapter 10

The Challenge of Our Desires

(and the deception that expects desires to bring happiness)

James 4:1-6

It's encouraging to talk about sowing seeds of righteousness (3:18) but now James pictures what we too often see, quarrels, fights, murder and coveting. He has already mentioned the possibility of a heart full of "bitter envy and self-seeking" which generates boasting and lying against the truth (3:14), but now he details what it produces, what we see in families and churches.

These verses explain the effect of the *bitter* stream. James asks, "does a spring send forth fresh water and bitter from the same opening" (3:11)? The answer is, "no, it doesn't." And when we see the talk of one who seems to be a Christian making havoc of community life, we know that there is something seriously polluted in the stream.

Talking about purity of speech doesn't necessarily result in purity of speech. Information by itself doesn't produce changes because becoming a doer of the word is more difficult than we think. It's not simply the addition of purity to our lives. There's also a subtraction part which involves getting rid of dirty hands and double-minded hearts. That's a large battle with entrenched habits and Satanic influence, which is only won by the kind of repentance James describes in verses 7-10.

Chapter 3 ended with the *wisdom from above*. This section adds a glimpse of what life is like that never finds such wisdom, and then explains in 4:7-10 the source of that purity which is so essential to wisdom.

I. The Source of Conflicts is Our Desires

Where do wars and fights come from among you? Do they not come from your desires for pleasure that war in your members? You lust and do not have. You murder and covet and cannot obtain. You fight and war. Yet you do not have because you do not ask. You ask and do not receive, because you ask amiss, that you may spend it on your pleasures (James 4:1-3).

The words *desires for pleasure* in verse 1 and *pleasures* in verse 3 come from the Greek word *hedona*, from which we get *hedonism*. The source of the campaigns that were splitting the church into different camps was a passion for *pleasure*, a totally different brand of wisdom from the one in 3:18 that pursues peace.

The word means *minty smell* or *sweet smell* and thus what delights. *Hedonism* is chasing whatever delights. It's the confidence that the only thing worth pursuing in life is pleasure, however one may define the concept.

It all starts with, "you lust." But the result is you "do not have" and "cannot obtain," and "do not receive." It doesn't work. But instead of saying, "maybe I will try something else," the poor hedonist tries harder, and adds more lust, and super lust, and war, and murder. Yet everything leads to complete emptiness.

Wars and fights are nothing more than one's pleasures on the rampage. These are people who have swallowed the world's world view. They're into parties and alcohol and drugs and sex and money and cars and things and extreme experiences for the highs they bring. They watch the glitter and glamour of life's stars and think that those people have it all! They're always smiling. After all, as the beer commercial once said, "it doesn't get any better than this." Once you believe that statement you chase what the world has to offer. Yet, the end result? *You do not have!*

We are told that the philosophy of *hedonism* was popularized by the ancient Greek philosopher Epicurus, who started a school in 307 BC and taught that our life's goal should be to minimize pain and maximize pleasure. It's any theory that gives pleasure the central role in life. In its simplest form it announces, "whatever brings pleasure is *right.*"

The philosophy is ridiculous to start with. Think of why it can never work. For example, "brings pleasure to whom?" Me? What if what brings pleasure to me hurts you? That might not be as good, so maybe we should say "brings pleasure to everyone." But who decides what best brings pleasure to everyone? And who knows what brings pleasure? And what is *pleasure*? Is smoking pleasure when we know that in twenty or thirty years it promises lung cancer? Do you see the impossible problems?

What happens is that hedonism has to stay a private philosophy because it will never work in a group. To live in a group, individuals need some concern for others. But once someone is committed to a personal goal of pleasure, the value of others diminishes.

Chapter 4 introduced my history in hedonism, how as a young Christian I wanted to serve God and study His Word and minister to others. At the same time I wanted to live for pleasure. I couldn't serve God without an airplane, and a boat, and a car. So down inside was a passion, a pride, a lust, an ego, an impatience that ruled my life, even as outwardly I was a nice Christian boy. At times it seemed that an army lived inside, trying to take over and convert me to total hedonism, trying to get me to give up on this serving God thing, just let it all hang out and live for pleasure.

At the same time there was the call of God in my heart that said, "all that other stuff that promises so much is just emptiness and depression; follow me and find life." I was just what James describes here, *double minded* (4:8). I wanted both. I wanted God, and I wanted the world. I was a fence rider. As a result I lived a roller coaster life where at times I was under the control of my desires, and at other times my desires were quieter, and I could with some calmness and logic think about what God wanted. Have you ever been there? That's the *hedona-wisdom* struggle, the fight between God and the world, summarized by Jesus in Matthew 6:24: "You cannot serve God and mammon."

Contrast this *hedona-wisdom* conflict with the wisdom in 3:17, that starts with *purity*. Here, the wisdom from this world is first of all *pleasure*. Both describe an inner dialog over one's ultimate goal in life. And the outcome is either *righteousness* (3:18) or *emptiness* (4:3).

II. Living for Pleasure Changes Us

I thought I could live for pleasure without it changing my heart. The pleasure life could be relegated to vacations, or late night splurges. The rest of the time I could be the normal me. But I found that to be difficult. Change was inevitable.

A. Desire becomes god. *"You lust and do not have. You murder and covet and cannot obtain. You fight and war. Yet you do not have because you do not ask" (James 4:2).*

The word *lust* is the word *desire*, the same word we saw in 1:14-15. Temptation comes when we are "drawn away" by our desires "and enticed." Then, desire "conceives," gives birth to "sin," and ultimately "brings forth death." Here we see that the hope which desire dangled in front of us was only a dream. We "do not have;" we "cannot obtain."

The two words that pinpoint the source of our problems are *desire* and *pleasure*. With these words as god, our lives cannot stay the same. They will change us completely, even to the place where we *murder, covet, fight,* and *war.* They will fill our hearts with a passion that has to *have*, has to *get*, has to *possess*, another car, another house, another money market fund, another wife or husband.

The words *fight and war* show that this is not a passive desire, a quiet strategy for something. The word *war* suggests a campaign, with all the planning and equipment to accomplish victory. Everything is designed for conquering. Personal power becomes more important because one must fight and brawl one's way to accomplish one's will. The competition may be a position in the choir or on the elder board, or Sunday school pins, or rewards for serving God, or it may result in cutting down each other with the tongue. But there's a battle going on because the desire has to have some minty-smelling thing.

B. Values in life change. It's like changing all the price tags in a store. All of the merchandise in your personal store gets jumbled. Once pleasure and possessions become number one all other values are re-distributed. It's like an excel program; you change one number in the upper left hand corner, and all the other numbers on the page change.

C. Relationships with people change. Other people become less valuable when desire takes over. They become tools to manipulate to accomplish one's will, even if it means fighting, quarreling, and, yes, murder. Would Christians actually get to murder? Don't rule it out. Did you ever read what the man after God's own heart did when he became hedonistic? I'm thinking of David and Bathsheba. But even if James doesn't have actual murder in mind here, there's the metaphorical murder Jesus spoke of in Matthew 5:22, the bitter hatred that sees no value in the life of a brother. Desire can run over people.

D. Relationship with God changes. Another sad effect of pleasure ruling our hearts is that prayer becomes a tool to pry what we want out of God. *"Yet you do not have because you do not ask. You ask and do not receive, because you ask amiss, that you may spend it on your pleasures" (vv. 2b-3).* We try to formulate our prayers in a way that pulls the wool over God's eyes in order to make Him our servant!

Two words emphasize the striking horror of this prayer. The word *amiss* means "sick." Our requests are sick. We calculate, "how can I pray, what special words can I choose to get God to give me what I want?" Books are written to help here. Sometimes special catchwords are recommended, or praying louder with more zeal, or praying with authority, or praying as if these things belong to me already as the King's child. Sometimes it's the quantity of prayer that is emphasized, praying thru until God obeys you. Are you familiar with those tactics? They're sick.

The simple fact is that prayer is God's means of fellowship. It's the way we develop *a relationship,* the way we fellowship, not the way we get something out of Him. How would you like it if your husband, wife, friend, child, only talked with you when they wanted to get something out of you? Have you ever had those kinds of friendships? They tend to make you sick, like desire-driven-wisdom does to God.

The other word is *spend,* the same word used to describe what the prodigal son did with his inheritance. He squandered it. Here desire-driven Christians are fervently praying, asking things of God in order to squander them, splurge them on their commitment to pleasure.

Think about how sinners who have made thousands of mistakes and bad choices will go to God, who has never made one mistake, never made a bad choice, and say to Him, "I have a better idea on this one, and I want You to change Your mind and do my plan." Have you ever told God how to answer your prayer? That probably sounds to God like a five-year-old trying to tell his father how to fix the car.

But for some reason we are quite confident that we know what is needed. As a result, we often don't go to God to pray and fellowship; we go *to take over!* Our prayers become nothing more than a strategic campaign to impose our will on God, to make Him our *servant!* Do you see why James uses the word *sick?*

The appropriate attitude in prayer must always be: "Our Father, Who art in heaven; hallowed be Thy name; Thy kingdom come, Thy will be done." That's the prayer of one who realizes the huge gulf between himself and the perfect God, realizes that he is the five-year-old, and focuses his prayer on God's name, God's kingdom, and the accomplishment of God's will.

What are God's interests? Paul directs us to pray for leaders of countries and for all people everywhere because God wants them saved (1 Timothy 2:1-4). We should pray for the peace of Jerusalem because God wants the city and the nation to experience His peace (Psalm 122:6). We should pray for our growth in Christ because God has predestined us to become "holy and without blame" (Ephesians 1:4). We should pray that our church experiences revival and the filling of the presence of God because God wants to fill His temple (Ephesians 3:19). Our requests need to be, *Thy will, Thy kingdom, Thy name* centered.

The truth is that God knows what is best for us; His will is good and acceptable and perfect, *absolutely perfect!* David Jeremiah says it well: "If we really believe that the will of God is perfect, then why would we want Him to change it?"[27] That's a great question. Isn't that the point in prayer? God's will is perfect! To think that I could improve on it is sheer idiotic pride. Why would I ever go to God and present an alternative plan to what is *perfect?* Why would anyone think their notions are better? It's nothing but desire-driven sin that causes us to question whether God's will is the best thing for us.

III. Living for Pleasure Drains Life from our Lives

Adulterers and adulteresses! Do you not know that friendship with the world is enmity with God? Whoever therefore wants to be a friend of the world makes himself an enemy of God. Or do you think that the Scripture says in vain, "The Spirit who dwells in us yearns jealously"? But He gives more grace. Therefore He says: "God resists the proud, But gives grace to the humble" (James 4:4-6).

Hedonism promises *life* and *happiness* at the same time that it attacks the very foundations of life and happiness.

A. It breaks our marriage relationship with God. *"Adulterers and adulteresses!" (v. 4).* Why would James call these people by such strong names? Because their relationship with God has changed.

What happens when a husband becomes an adulterer? He may be living with his wife, but he becomes an adulterer? What changes? He may live and work at the same place. Everything outwardly may look normal. But his relationship with his wife has been broken.

The same awful thing happens in our relationship with God when we come to the incredibly wrong conclusion that God is *not sufficient.* Our desires convince us that God cannot provide for our happiness needs and we have to turn somewhere else, like the world. We're sleeping with the enemy by concluding that the world is greater than God. We've become adulterers and adulteresses.

At what point does this relational disaster begin? "Whoever therefore *wants* to be a friend of the world makes himself an enemy of God." Even *before* one signs up as a card-carrying friend of the world. Outwardly nothing may change. But he *wants* it. It's *the desire to befriend the world* that breaks one's relationship with God, just like the husband breaks his relationship with his wife as soon as he wants the other woman.

B. It breaks the heart of God. *"The Spirit who dwells in us yearns jealously"? (v. 5).* This verse is translated different ways because it's not clear what the subject is. The New American Standard Bible, for example, translates it, "He jealously desires the Spirit which He has made to dwell in us." That makes God the subject. The New King James version translates it, "the Spirit who dwells in us yearns jealously." That makes the indwelling Spirit the subject, which I think is better. The New International Version is similar, "the spirit he caused to live in us envies intensely." The sentence introduces us to the effect our turn to worldliness has on the indwelling Holy Spirit. And the description is, *jealously desires* or *yearns jealously* or *envies intensely.*

We are told that one of the greatest psychological and emotional pains is to be double crossed by someone you truly love and have committed yourself to. Can you imagine what it's like to give your only Son to die for someone else, give that person millions of dollars' worth of blessings, bring that person into your own home and family, and then hear the person say, "no thanks, I'd rather go back to my sin." God watches His children turn to the world like the father in Luke 15 watched His prodigal son leave, with tears. What a tragedy!

And what does this pleasure-driven wisdom supply for the Christian?

C. It supplies complete emptiness. *"You desire and do not have, so you murder. You covet and cannot obtain, so you fight and quarrel. You do not have, because you do not ask. You ask and do not receive, because you ask wrongly, to spend it on your passions" (James 4:2-3 ESV).*

The phrases "do not have," "cannot obtain," "do not have," and "do not receive" describe a life of *frustration*. After you have obeyed your passions, plans, and purposes, you always come out empty. You run and work and fight and chase and collapse in a heap, all tired out, with nothing. It's a giant Ponzi scheme – you invest your life cash and it disappears. It promises much; it's going to have a great return and looks good for the first months, but you wake up a year later with zero.

The desire-driven life seems to turn you into a porcupine chasing balloons. Just as you almost get what you desire it disappears with a pop. How tragic, to invest the time, energy and wisdom God gives us, into *nothing*.

If you are living for pleasure as the ultimate goal in life, when are you going to stop? What do you want, more nothing? Now is the time to break the chain, to interrupt the pattern. If you don't do it now, chances are slim that you will do it in the future.

IV. God Wants to *Give* Us What Pleasure Only Promises

The amazing thing is that God *has already promised* what the world offers, only in a different and better way.

A. Desire-driven wisdom has only words. It says, "follow me to real life." Christ says, "I am the bread of life" (John 6:35). James gives this amazing promise: "But He gives more grace. Therefore He says: 'God resists the proud, But gives grace to the humble'" (4:6).

God gives grace! What kind of grace? The kind you have been looking for out in the world. Only a better kind, the kind you really wanted and were praying for, but you didn't understand what it was, so your were trying to manipulate God for stuff you could squander on your pleasures. The simple truth is that God has everything you need for a totally blessed life, and He wants to *give it to you*.

False teachers picture this promise of grace as a credit card that can get us anything we want. "After all," they say, "delight yourself also in the LORD, And He shall give you the desires of your heart"

(Psalm 37:4). In other words, if you follow their method, He will give you that new Corvette, that beautiful or handsome new mate, that huge home, and the boat. What they do is play on one's desire for pleasure.

Isn't that what the text says? No, it's not what the text says. In fact James 4:4 specifically says that they ask and *don't* receive because they ask *wrongly*, with the motive of spending it on their pleasures. Once pleasure becomes part of the prayer equation, the prayer insults God. It turns Him into the genie-in-the-bottle who obeys us. The truth is that God wants to give us the happiness and joy *without the things that pleasure demands*.

In fact, the amazing testimony of Christians who know is that God can give us the happiness with *nothing else* except the presence of God. The psalmist discovered this: "In Your presence *is* fullness of joy; At Your right hand *are* pleasures forevermore" (Psalm 16:11). Think of that, "fullness of joy," in *His presence*. Just being in His presence will so fill your joy tank, that you will look at all the treasures the world has to offer as trash and plastic jewelry. The psalmist then adds, "pleasures forevermore," eternal pleasures, non-ending delights, repeated excitement at His right hand!

Have you ever experienced the absolute thrill of being in God's presence? If you have never experienced that, it will be pretty hard to stay away from *hedona* type wisdom. The world's offerings look pretty tempting to those who know nothing of God's incredible presence.

B. God's gifts come in response to fellowship. *"Yet you do not have because you do not ask" (v. 2)*. We live on *empty* because we don't ask! Unfulfilled emptiness, even with all the things we Americans pile up because we do not spent time with God the giver of "every good and every perfect gift" (James 1:17). We don't ask because we don't trust God. We want Him to do it our way. When He doesn't we can't wait because we're not sure, and the lights of the world grow brighter.

Our daughter met a beggar on the streets of Calcutta, India, that impacted her life. His name was Stephen. He had one leg missing and thus could not work. He lived with his wife and four children in a cardboard box. What was so striking to my daughter was how happy he was in Jesus Christ. He was excited about what Christ had done for him. One day she brought him a small meal. He ate a little bit, and refused to eat the rest, because he wanted to take it home to his cardboard box and enjoy it with his family. He was starving, and yet he was so happy to share his food with his children. If beggars on the streets of Calcutta can find the joy of the Lord, why can't American Christians who have a thousand times as much stuff as Stephen will ever have?

God's wisdom begins with *purity* and *contentment*. "And having food and raiment let us be therewith content" (1 Timothy 6:6 KJV). Are you content? Or are you still chasing after your pleasure desires? If so, you are foolish. And if you are a real Christian, you will weep in eternity when you realize what you gave in trade for your storage units full of emptiness.

Chapter 11

The Challenge of Humility
(and the deception that supposes we're OK)

James 4:7-10

Old Testament prophets had been preaching "repentance" for years. When Isaiah prophesied, "'Come now, and let us reason together,' Says the LORD, 'Though your sins are like scarlet, They shall be as white as snow; Though they are red like crimson, They shall be as wool'" (1:18), he was calling for repentance. When Jonah entered Nineveh and said, "Forty days and this city will be dust," he was calling for repentance.

John the Baptist came preaching, "repent for the kingdom of heaven is here." Jesus began preaching, "repent for the kingdom of heaven is here." The disciples were sent out preaching, "repent for the kingdom of heaven is here." Over and over again God has called for repentance.

But what does it mean to repent? People think of it as *changing your mind and going in a different direction.* That's true. But what does that mean in real life? John the Baptist expected people to confess their sins and get baptized, which was a public statement that they were in sin and, like Gentiles, needed to re-enter the family of Israel. Jesus and His disciples expected the same thing.

That definition of repentance is kind of strange in today's thinking because we see it as something *private*, that you might indicate by raising a finger, signing a card, or wiping a tear from your eye. Maybe that's partly why our repentance fails to change much. Maybe it's not repentance. The difficulty of repentance is that it is *humbling*. We will do yards of work to keep from having to humble ourselves.

Verse 6 ended with the promise that God wants to give us the fulfillment we so vainly chase by our desires. But is God's grace for everyone? No, it says, "but gives grace to the humble." The testimony of all Scripture is that God pays special attention to the humble.

For example: "For thus says the High and Lofty One Who inhabits eternity, whose name is Holy: 'I dwell in the high and holy place, With him who has a contrite and humble spirit, To revive the spirit of the humble, And to revive the heart of the contrite ones'" (Isaiah 57:15).

"For the LORD takes pleasure in His people; He will beautify the humble with salvation" (Psalm 149:4).

"The humble He guides in justice, And the humble He teaches His way" (Psalm 25:9).

"Then he said to me, 'Do not fear, Daniel, for from the first day that you set your heart to understand, and to humble yourself before your God, your words were heard; and I have come because of your words'" (Daniel 10:12). Even Daniel, the man of God, humbled himself!

Is it any surprise, then, that this section ends with the command, "Humble yourselves in the sight of the Lord, and He will lift you up." James is writing to people who are trying to lift themselves up by chasing their desires for pleasure. Even though God wants to give them grace they truly need, they won't find it until they humble themselves.

What does it mean to humble ourselves? James explains it with ten commands that summarize the repentance/humility package. Here are the commands: "*Therefore* **submit** *to God.* **Resist** *the devil and* *he will flee from you.* **Draw near** *to God and He will draw near to you.* **Cleanse your hands**, *you sinners; and* **purify your hearts**, *you double-minded.* **Lament** *and* **mourn** *and* **weep!** **Let your laughter be turned to mourning** *and your joy to gloom.* **Humble yourselves** *in the sight of the Lord, and He will lift you up."*

Let me summarize the commands in five categories:

I. Choose sides

"Therefore submit to God. Resist the devil and he will flee from you" (v. 7). What would the wife say to her adulterous husband? "Choose her or me." The wife is jealous. A marriage relationship is exclusive. The same with God. He said to the nation of Israel when she turned to adultery. "You can't sit on the fence; you can't stay in the embrace of two; you can't serve God and mammon; you only think you can; and that's your problem."

> And if it seems evil to you to serve the LORD, choose
> for yourselves this day whom you will serve, whether the
> gods which your fathers served that were on the other side
> of the River, or the gods of the Amorites, in whose land
> you dwell. But as for me and my house, we will serve the
> LORD (Joshua 24:15)

"And Elijah came to all the people, and said, How long will you falter between two opinions? If the LORD is God, follow Him; but if Baal, follow him" (1 Kings 18:21).

The first part of the command is, "submit to God." The word actually means, "to line yourself up under the authority of someone." Get in line with the intention of obeying and supporting someone, the sergeant, the boss, the president, the leader. Since God *resists* the proud (v. 6) you don't want to live there. You want to submit to His direction.

The issue here is your *will*. My will or His will? Who's in charge? Who calls the shots? Who's making the decisions? We pray and say, Thy kingdom come, Thy will be done on earth as it is done in heaven."

How is God's will accomplished in heaven? "Bless the LORD, you His angels, Who excel in strength, who do His word, Heeding the voice of His word" (Psalm 103:20). There are no questions about obedience in heaven. The angels instantly run to do what God desires.

Why would we not want to do it that way? Since God's plan is perfect, since God knows what's best, since every good and perfect gift comes from above, why wouldn't we want to obey exactly? It makes no sense to resist the best thing for us.

The second part of the command tells us where our resistance needs to be placed: *"Resist the devil."* "Resist" and "submit" are opposites. In order to submit to God you have to stand against all the other choices. Doing one involves doing the other. Obeying God means disobeying Satan. The proper response to Satan is "NO." Whether he allures you, or flatters you, or tempts you, or threatens you, the only response is, *no.*

As the father of lies (John 8:44), Satan talks much stronger than he really is. He covers his true weakness, his true bankruptcy with enticing words. This command has an awesome assumption in it. *It assumes that we are capable of resisting the devil!*

The truth is that we are standing against a liar. He poses as powerful, wise and insightful, but he really has little authority or power. Even though it doesn't feel like it, even though our desires sometimes make us feel like it's impossible to say *no,* we're not helpless. We're not just bystanders, watching Satan do his thing in our lives.

God the Holy Spirit has already enabled us to stand. He has already supplied His armor, which can completely protect us. He has given us His Word, and we have seen a demonstration of how it completely protected Jesus in temptation. That Word has complete power to neutralize and defeat Satan's best temptations. This command is encouraging. James says, "step up to the plate against Satan's pitches, and hit a home run, by saying *no*."

Have you ever said, "I am on God's side exclusively? I am presenting my total being to Him? I want nothing to do with Satan's offers." Do that with all your heart.

II. Chase after Him

"Draw near to God and He will draw near to you" (v. 8). How do you get back into fellowship with God? Take the initiative and go after Him. He hasn't moved and He promises that He will be found when His people seek Him with all their hearts.

> "For I know the thoughts that I think toward you, says the LORD, thoughts of peace and not of evil, to give you a future and a hope. Then you will call upon Me and go and pray to Me, and I will listen to you. And you will seek Me and find Me, when you search for Me with all your heart. I will be found by you, says the LORD . . ." (Jeremiah 29:11-14).

Observe the amazing promises: "I will listen to you" (v. 12); "You will seek Me and find Me" (v. 13); "I will be found by you" (v. 14). That's exactly what James is saying with "draw near."

The conjunction *and* usually connects two clauses that are of roughly equal weight. "You draw near" *and* "He will draw near." If you don't draw near, *He still might draw near*, although we don't know that for sure. But beyond a shadow of a doubt, when you draw near, *He for certain will reciprocate.* The word *and* (along with the verb *will*) makes God's presence a promise, a wonderful promise.

Do you feel distant from God? Go after Him! God says, "the ball is in your court; you've got to make the first move." He draws near to us *after* we make the first move. And if He is not in our lives it's because we haven't drawn near.

How does one draw near? People say, "I read the Bible and pray and nothing happens." Well what did you do when you drew near to *the world*? Did you think about it? Listen to it's promises again and again? What did you do when you first fell in love? How did you *draw near*? Probably some of you were quite clever, designing creative ways of getting the other person's attention, finding excuses to meet. You probably put a considerable amount of time and effort into setting things up. Have you done that with God?

My dating days were not known for my cleverness or ability to sweep women off their feet. One of the girls I was interested in gave up on me in anger because, among other things, I showed up very late for a date. I took a beautiful young lady to the New York World's Fair in 1964 intending to continue the relationship. But she ended it with an invitation to her wedding several years later.

Why have I enjoyed married life with Martha for more than fifty years? A big part of it was that she knew this clumsy guy was trying to *draw near.* And she felt sorry for him, even as she laughed. I think God is like Martha. He knows our hearts, and even when we don't do it very well, He knows when we really want Him.

I would encourage you to go to Him as best you know how. Talk to Him and say, "God, I have moved, and I'm a long way away from You. And You've invited me to come to you. I don't really know how to do that. But whatever that means, I want to do it. Would you forgive my sin and my distance from you? Would you enable me to draw near to you in honesty of heart, and submit and obey?"

And I would stay on my knees in prayer, pursuing God and asking for His help, until something happens. I find that when God draws near, His qualities affect me, with peace, and joy, and love, and gentleness. There is a lightness that comes into my life, a wholeness that quiets all the things that cause me such fretting.

I find that to consistently draw near to God I need to schedule it. Schedule a time to read Scripture, schedule a time to pray whether you want to or not. The psalmist says, "Seven times a day I praise You, Because of Your righteous judgments" (Psalm 119:164). Think of that schedule. How do you find and fit seven slots for praise into your daily schedule? The psalmist couldn't leave things to when *he felt like it*. He knew he might not feel like it.

III. Clean up your life

"Cleanse your hands, you sinners; and purify your hearts, you double-minded" (v. 8). Their hands made them sinners. "Hands" represent the outside, what you do, what you say to others, the lying, the fighting, the hurting, the ignoring, the degrading of others. "Hearts" represents the inside, the mind and the conversations, which are double-minded. Both of these guide us in sin.

The two words, *sinners* and *double-minded*, are a smack in the face. James is calling his readers low down sinners and two faced hypocrites. A hypocrite is an actor or actress, posing as someone they are not, acting as if they are interested when they aren't, acting like church is an important part of their lives when in reality it's a bother. Jewish people in New Testament times detested hypocrisy, and viewed hypocrites as some of the lowest of people, down there with the tax collectors.

Hypocrites say the right things, go through the right motions, but their minds are somewhere else. They are double-minded and secretly in love with the world. They can pray all they want, sing all they want, give all they want, but God knows their hearts. Friendship with God awaits their confession.

There's an incredible power in a secret. Satan uses secrets to control us. That's why God comands us to confess and admit. Confession is for our benefit. You don't think it informs God of anything do you? The only release from the power of the secret is full confession of it. That's the point in these two commands to *cleanse* and *purify*.

I once caught the story on the radio of a couple in crisis. He was a traveling salesman who had become unfaithful to his wife. He had an adulterous lifestyle with women in several different cities to which he traveled. He was miserable, he was caught, he admitted his sin, and he and his wife began working on restoration. Their book *Beyond Affairs* describes hours of talking, and years of dealing with correlating issues that came up.[28] The talking and confession were not for the purpose of getting forgiveness. She had already granted that. It was for the purpose of restoring their relationship to the place where they could trust each other again and live together as one. If I remember correctly, he said they talked it out for two years. But his conclusion? His relationship with his wife was now ten times better than anything he ever had when running around with all the other women.

That's the point: confess it, admit it to everyone you sinned against; tell them all you can remember about what you thought and did in all of its gory detail. Don't hold anything back. James says, "Confess your trespasses to one another, and pray for one another, that you may be healed" (5:16). He's not talking about announcing all your sins to the world but confessing to those who have been affected and getting them to pray for you. The apostle John adds this promise, "if we confess our sins, He is faithful and just to forgive us our sins, and to cleanse us from all unrighteousness" (1 John 1:9).

IV. Weep over your loss

"Lament and mourn and weep! Let your laughter be turned to mourning and your joy to gloom" (v. 9). There are four commands in this verse, "lament," "mourn," "weep," and "turned."

To have these commands right after the word, *double-minded* is significant. The double minded person is someone who is quite capable of weeping and mourning and lamenting, *and faking it.* But the command is to genuinely lament and mourn and weep, in a way that turns even laughter into gloom. Why?

These emotions arise from a recognition of what you have done. They come from understanding God's incredible love and sacrifice, and the realization that your double mindedness has turned you away from the only real love you will ever experience.

Think of a teenager who gets drunk, drives his car down the sidewalk, runs over and kills a six year old boy. He repents, he asks everyone involved to forgive him, he goes to prison. So far so good. What he needs to do is understand his actions from the perspective of the parents who lost the six year old. They are weeping. Their loss will never return. The teen needs to weep with the parents and come to their understanding of his actions.

Jesus said, "blessed are those who mourn." Why? What do they mourn over? Their sin. The time, the life they have wasted, both gifts from God. This doesn't mean to inflict pain on yourself. This isn't penance, where you punish yourself to pay for your sin. God forgives when we confess and forsake but getting free from our sin includes mourning over it.

"Let your laughter be turned to mourning and your joy to gloom" commands us to express deep grief and sorrow, like the shock of having someone close to you pass away suddenly.

The same is true in your relationship with God. This command is based on understanding how amazing and rare that relationship was. What's it like to lose a good friend? Your mom or dad? How about a son or daughter? That's the loss of something so precious that you can't cry enough, you can't get the pain of the missing relationship out of your system.

"Let your laughter be turned" suggests what happens when we walk into a funeral home. All of a sudden there is a different atmosphere. People talk quietly. There are Kleenex boxes on almost every table. It's a place of death, weeping, and mourning.

Think of the worst funeral you ever experienced, a loss so great you couldn't stop crying, couldn't get the hole it left in your heart fixed. And you still don't know what to do. It jumbles the rest of your life and leaves you in a daze.

That's the picture of sin's toll. Unbelievable loss. Throwing away a relationship with the King of kings and Lord of lords, the One who so loved you that He died for you. And you have chosen someone else and become the adulterer or adulteress. Mourning is part of coming to understand the horror of what you have done.

V. Humble yourself

"Humble yourselves in the sight of the Lord, and He will lift you up" (v. 10). The act of humbling yourself is the root from which the other nine commands develop. And the other nine commands are the essential characteristics of humility.

What is humility? What do these nine commands do to humble us? First they change our relationship with God. Satan will flee (v. 7); God will draw near to us (v. 8). They also will change the way we talk to ourselves, our inner dialog. And that may be a helpful way to think about the word "humility." It's talking to ourselves with a deep sense of our littleness.[29]

"A deep sense of our littleness" affects the choices we make. We can choose the lower road rather than the upper road. We can choose to serve rather than get served (Mark 10:43-44). We can choose to associate with the humble (Romans 12:16), and invite to dinner widows and orphans who can't pay us back (Luke 14:13-14).

It's that "deep sense of littleness," that "contrite and humble spirit" (Isaiah 57:15) that God has promised to bless. Jesus said, "Whoever exalts himself will be humbled, and whoever humbles himself will be exalted" (Matthew 23:12). God can only exalt the humble and supply their need of grace. He has committed Himself to this mode of action. He cannot exalt the proud, no matter how smart, rich, educated they may be, no matter how many years of Bible study they may have had.

What does true repentance look like? Humbling one's self as we've seen in these four directives: (a) choosing sides, getting off the fence and rejecting the devil and his offers; (b) chasing after God, drawing near to Him in the best way you know; (c) cleansing your hands and heart by confessing and straightening out everything you have done; and (d) crying and mourning over your loss. God promises to respond to this kind of repentance, with Grace! Two things in closing:

A. These commands describe our responsibilities. They are all voluntary. James doesn't say, "pray for God to humble you." God wants to lift you up when you obey these commands. No one can make you do these directions. Repentance is one hundred percent our responsibility. We do it ourselves. Jesus said, "if you know these things, happy are you if you do them" (John 13:17).

B. God's goal is to "lift us up." The commands result in God supplying Grace to us, God lifting us up. Lift us up in the sense of bringing us back into that intimate communion with Him that makes life worthwhile! God is saying to people, who like the prodigal son have made shambles of their lives, who have sold themselves to the highest pleasure, "return to Me; I want to forgive you and lift you back up into fellowship with Me." What a promise! What a God!

Chapter 12

The Challenge of Pride

(and the deception that ignores one's insignificance)

James 4:11-17

If humility involves "a deep sense of our littleness," the people James has in mind in this section haven't yet developed humility. In fact the littleness they see only belongs to those around them.

Jesus gave a parable in Luke 18 of two men who went up to pray, a Pharisee and a publican. Luke introduced the story by saying, "He spoke this parable to some who trusted in themselves that they were righteous, and despised others." The combination, "trusted in themselves and despised others" also fits the deception in this passage. Both the negative attitude toward others in verses 11-12 and the arrogant self confidence in verses 13-17 arise from pride, and come as a contrast to the humility commanded in verses 7-10. Somehow humans have the ability to talk down others while featuring their own ambitious plans. This is not just talking evil, but thinking evil and thinking that it's OK to think this way.

I. Trash Talk is Dangerous

Do not speak evil of one another, brethren. He who speaks
evil of a brother and judges his brother, speaks evil of the

*law and judges the law. But if you judge the law, you are not
a doer of the law but a judge. There is one Lawgiver, who is
able to save and to destroy. Who are you to judge another?
(James 4:11-12).*

The words *speak evil* mean "to talk against," or "to talk down." They refer to words that undermine, criticize, defame, usually someone who is absent.

Sometimes we talk this way as a joke. Such joking is harmless *as long as nothing else is intended.* The problem comes when we pose as if we are kidding others when we really intend to put them down. That's where evil appears.

Speak evil appears three times in verse 11. *Judge* appears four times and once in verse 12. Speech turns evil when the heart makes a judgment about another. It's the thinking that preceded the usher's choice in 2:1-3, and the man facing a hungry brother and sister in 2:15-16, and the person in 3:9 who can simultaneously bless God and curse someone made in the image of God. It's the heart James described in 3:14-16 and the resulting chaos of 4:1-3.

What makes this kind of thinking and talking so dangerous? James lists four causes:

A. It attacks family. *Brothers* implies that they are speaking about fellow believers. This is family talk. And it seems that our tongues get a little looser when we speak of our own brothers and sisters. When growing up did you speak of your siblings in careful, reverent terms? Or did you feel free to criticize them and let others know their weaknesses?

It's not only an issue of how we talk about someone, but what we intend. The motive behind the words is important. You can say something that may sound complementary, but the way you say it, the motive with which you say it, digs at the other person. Some people can do this with almost everyone they know. They even can give praise in a negative way.

For example: "my, that's a great-looking dress. Too bad they didn't have your size." "Why waste time practicing? You'll never play the piano like your sister." "Wow, you look marvelous! Did you have plastic surgery?" When a man finally got up the nerve to tell his mother that his wife had left him, his mother snapped, "What took her so long?"

Contrast this talk with the way we speak of, let's say, the astronauts in the Challenger disaster, or the Columbia shuttle disaster. We speak with honor, respect, reverence and appreciation. People would be insulted if someone tried to trash talk them. What's wrong with talking that way about every person, especially a brother and sister in Christ?

Someone has said, "strong minds discuss ideas, average minds discuss events, weak minds discuss people."[30] Lack of respect for others coupled with an inflated trust in ourselves tend to make us experts at generalization. A brother says a foolish word, and we say, "he never says anything valuable." A sister gets angry and loses her temper, and we say, "she is always out of control." Someone fails to greet us in the way we expect, and we classify him as "unfriendly."

How dangerous is this kind of talk? Everybody does it. It's all-American entertainment. But James reacts like a situation I was in recently. I was filling up a two gallon plastic gas can at the gas station. A man drove up in a pickup close to the other side of the pump and got out smoking a cigarette. The lighted end was probably less than four feet from the opening of my gas can. I thought, "he's going to blow up this can. What should I do? Should I pull the hose out and put it back in the pump? Would that cause more vapors? Should I shove it further into the can?" I did the later, and wanted to say, "What are you doing?" "Are you trying to kill yourself and me?"

That's what James feels here: "what are you doing? Are you trying to kill the family of God?"

B. It attacks the Law. *"He who speaks evil of a brother and judges his brother, speaks evil of the law and judges the law" (James 4:11).*

What law is James talking about? The ten commandments? No, I think it's the law he mentioned in 2:8, the royal law, the law of love. God's law says "love your brother," "love your neighbor." That law commands us to help our brother or sister. But by judging another, we say in effect, "that law doesn't fit this person," or maybe, "this person isn't worth the effort."

Peter says that "love will cover a multitude of sins" (I Peter 4:8). But we respond with, "not in this case." "This brother needs his sins exposed." Trash talk judging doesn't obey the command to love. Its actions criticize the law. It's not submitting and obeying the law, but setting itself above it in order to push it aside.

Have you ever *talked down* teenagers? Or older people? Or those who pull out in front of you driving slowly? Or people who look weird? Or are different? Have you ever talked down Calvinists? Or Arminians? Or Amillennialists? Or Charismatics? Or used car salesmen? Does God's law cover our response to them? Of course! Especially if they are family.

Disobedience to the law of love is an attack on the law, exalting yourself above it by telling yourself that you can decide when it applies.

C. It turns the talker into a JUDGE. *"He who speaks evil of a brother and judges his brother, speaks evil of the law and judges the law. But if you judge the law, you are not a doer of the law but a judge" (James 4:11).*

The act of talking down your brother is the act of setting yourself up as an authority. A judge has to know much in order to make a good judgment. You, by opening your mouth against a brother, show that you think you know enough to make your pronouncement.

It's a great temptation when you learn and grow a little as a believer, to assume an authoritative attitude toward other Christians. By doing this, we commonly assume responsibilities that belong to

God. Paul cautions us: "Therefore judge nothing before the time, until the Lord comes, who will both bring to light the hidden things of darkness and reveal the counsels of the hearts. Then each one's praise will come from God" (1 Corinthians 4:5).

I have had training in public speaking and have taught college level introductory courses for fifty years. I have evaluated thousands and thousands of speeches and sermons. How easy it is for me to criticize preachers. Yet the truth is that I don't know enough to judge. I have no idea as to how many obstacles they have overcome in their lives. They may have been born without the ability to speak like Helen Keller and have overcome far more difficulties than I will ever see. Who am I to judge? There is too much that is unseen and unknown. There are definite ways I can help students improve, and I do that, but I always need to be careful of the position I take as an instructor.

D. It invades God's courtroom to take over. *"There is one Lawgiver, who is able to save and to destroy. Who are you to judge another?" (James 4:12).*

In the entire universe, there is *one Lawgiver!* That is, until recently. And you, by your mouth have added yourself to that list of one. God has His own private courtroom where He judges cases and gives out the Law. And you have joined Him, for the specific purpose of attacking one of His special creations. His view is that He did a good job with His creation, but you think otherwise.

And you have hastily assembled judgment day in order to deal with this brother of yours. His fault needs to be exposed; he needs to be publicly embarrassed, and you are God's vessel to accomplish this act. God's law commands you love him (and cover a multitude of sins), but since you're superior to that law, you set up your own trial date.

James says, *"who do you think you are?"* You are assigning yourself a place on the throne of God that is already competently occupied.

What laws have you authored? What ability do you have to save and/or destroy? Your assignment from above is to join your brother to help him, stand beside your neighbor to strengthen her, to be a humble doer of the law. *Who do you think you are?*

Trash talk is serious stuff. It's a lighted cigarette getting awfully close to an open gas can. It's not another form of Christian entertainment. It attacks family, it sets aside the law, the person assumes the position of a judge, and invades God's rightful place. There's nothing minor about this kind of talk. It's Satanic.

The apostle Paul said, "Let no corrupt word proceed out of your mouth, but what is good for necessary edification, that it may impart grace to the hearers" (Ephesians 4:29).

II. Planning can get sinful

> Come now, you who say, "Today or tomorrow we will go to such and such a city, spend a year there, buy and sell, and make a profit"; whereas you do not know what will happen tomorrow. For what is your life? It is even a vapor that appears for a little time and then vanishes away. Instead you ought to say, "If the Lord wills, we shall live and do this or that." But now you boast in your arrogance. All such boasting is evil. Therefore, to him who knows to do good and does not do it, to him it is sin (James 4:13-17).

Notice the description, "today, tomorrow, a year." These were businessmen who had their schedules set. They knew where they were going to be and what they were going to do for the next year. They had the city chosen, and they were sure they could come back with full wallets.

Their talk is full of confidence. "We will go . . . spend a year there . . . buy and sell." They knew what to do. They had already filled in their tax returns for next year. It wasn't "let's try to make a profit." It was "we will make one," emphasizing their confidence in their ability. The word for "making a profit," not only includes making money, but the love of making money. Business projects like this were part of their DNA.

Remember that James is writing to Jewish people. Have you ever seen any Jewish people who don't know how to trade and make money? They are so good at it that it's natural to be confident. I wish I had that ability. They loved trade and could make it pay. Travel and trade were important parts of the Roman empire, and Jewish businessmen and women kept it going, as they still do today.

What's the problem with these statements? They sound like normal business life. Isn't this regular American planning? These guys may seem a little too confident, but nothing you'd want to make a federal case over. Why does James view their kind of planning as evil? What is it about these plans that makes them wrong?

A. The problem is an arrogance that focuses on the wrong thing. The key is the phrase, "boasting in your arrogance." "Boasting" is the word, *glorying* which we saw in 1:9. It can be good or bad boasting. But the word *arrogance* means, "an insolent and empty assurance, which trusts in its own power and resources," ignoring God's laws and human rights. It's sometimes translated by the word, *swagger*.[31] Just like the judge in verses 11-12, it's a swagger based on ignorance and pride; a large confidence in one's ability to handle everything around him, when he can't handle himself.

These guys act as if they have the future under control, they have figured out how to stay alive, how to design, build, sell products and how to make money, ignoring the fact that they have stage four cancer! It's all an empty display. They only have the future under control because they're ignorant of what's involved.

What's wrong is not just the planning, but *the arrogance that leaves out what's more important!* It's like a guy who decides to climb the corporate ladder, at the expense of his wife and family. His wife feels alone as the family grows because he is not there. But he is providing for their needs. And he keeps thinking that it will just be a few more years and he will be at the top. Then he can level off and have more time.

He finally arrives at leadership, and the seven plus figure salary. It's a nice ceremony that emphasizes how much he has contributed to the success of the company. His wife is there with the children, and they all go home proud of his accomplishments. On the drive home he is killed in a freak three-car collision. He leaves his wife in a nice house with four children, all well provided for, but virtually unaware of who their father was.

What has he accomplished? He has provided. That is a commendable thing. What else? Not much else. He knew there were other things he should be doing, but he excused them with the thought that for the moment he needed to make a secure future his priority.

We have an entire generation that lives in this realm: "let's collect the cash, let's get our retirement set up and filled, let's work for the company that pays the most no matter how great the sacrifice; let's seek first the money and all the things money will add." All the while God says, "seek first the kingdom of heaven and all these [other] things will be added" (Matthew 6:33).

How many parents don't have time for their children because they have to keep up with the Joneses? How many students can't finance their education because they have to buy a new car? It's sacrificing what's important for trinkets.

B. The problem is an arrogance that overlooks reality. When making money becomes the priority, other priorities have to drop out. How does God want us to plan for the future?

1. We should plan in light of our *frailty*. We are as permanent as *mist "For what is your life? It is even a vapor that appears for a little time and then vanishes away"* (v. 14). People don't understand how fragile life is. It's not made of rock or iron, but *vapor*. It's as a watery mist. It appears; it vanishes. These Jewish businessmen were *denying their deaths*. They were living as if they were the Blue Ridge mountains.

How long does the vapor last that comes out of your mouth on a cold day? It appears as you breathe out, and then it disappears. In the great scheme of things, that's the picture of the permanence of our lives. What does this mean? It means that whatever is most important should be done now. "Don't boast of tomorrow; for you know not what a day may bring forth" (Psalm 27:1); "our days on earth are like a shadow" (1 Chronicles 29:15), "for my days vanish like smoke" (Psalm 102:3).

Moses said, "so teach us to number our days, that we may give a heart to wisdom" (Psalm 90:12). "So teach us" is a request for God to interfere in our lives to help us number our days that we might get a heart of wisdom. Why do we need to be taught to number our days when we walk on the graves of our fathers and mothers? Why do we have to be taught that we're standing in that exit line and may be the next one called? Somehow we don't learn from all the movement into eternity around us.

Would you change your plans in any way if you knew you were leaving for eternity tomorrow? Would you worry about making another dollar? Someone has said that they never heard anyone on their deathbed saying, "I spent too much time with my family and children; too much time in church with other believers; too much time in prayer and meditation." It always seems to be, "I spent too much time at work; too much time worrying about the things that weren't that important." *Oh to have that kind of insight before life ends.*

These businessmen were worrying about the future to such an extent that they were missing the present. They were putting off doing good. They were putting present responsibilities on hold for a year. James says "that's arrogance," "that's evil," because it is based on false assumptions, the assumption that you are going to live.

2. We should plan in light of our *ignorance*. *"Whereas you do not know what will happen tomorrow" (v. 14).* We can't see an hour ahead, let alone a day or a year. They are *ignoring their ignorance.* Tomorrow may prove to be another Nine-Eleven when we all sit around and watch the news in fear, and wonder what else may happen. We don't know.

Why were they so confident that circumstances weren't going to change, and terrorists weren't going to hit the city, and the stock market wasn't going to collapse? Jesus said, "Therefore do not worry about tomorrow, for tomorrow will worry about its own things. Sufficient for the day is its own trouble" (Matthew 6:34). Obey what you know are today's responsibilities.

3. We should plan in light of our complete *dependence*. *"Instead you ought to say, 'If the Lord wills, we shall live and do this or that'" (v. 15).* "If the Lord wills" means that we are dependent upon His choice; "we shall live" means that we are dependent on His supply of breath and life; "and do this or that" means that we are dependent on Him for strength and health. They were underestimating their weaknesses. They were ignoring the possibility of coming down with Lymes disease and suddenly having zero energy for anything.

Making money while failing to do the right thing is *sin*. There's usually something more important than making money. Paul said to Timothy:

> "Command those who are rich in this present age not to be haughty, nor to trust in uncertain riches but in the living God, who gives us richly all things to enjoy. Let them do good, that they be rich in good works, ready to give, willing to share, storing up for themselves a good

foundation for the time to come, that they may lay hold on eternal life (1 Timothy 6:17-19).

Is there someone you would like to thank before you die? Their influence on you has been valuable and you want to tell them, but never have. Will you write a thank you note this week? Is there someone you would like to get things straightened out with before you die? Perhaps you have sinned against them and want to confess it. Perhaps they have sinned against you and you want to confront them, but in fear have been putting it off. Do it today. Have you written a will? Don't assume you have months to write it.

"Therefore, to him who knows to do good and does not do it, to him it is sin" (v. 17). A student came to see me once with a very bitter attitude. I counseled her to deal with her attitude. She agreed but said that she had to go to class. I said, "no you don't. If you go to class with that attitude you won't get anything out of it. Go to your room, get on your knees and stay there until God changes your attitude." *If your attitude is not right, everything else you do is going to be wrong.* Even making money, or going to a class.

Chapter 13

The Challenge of Covetousness
(and the deception that views wealth as God's blessing)

James 5:1-6

Come now, you rich, weep and howl for your miseries that are coming upon you! Your riches are corrupted, and your garments are moth-eaten. Your gold and silver are corroded, and their corrosion will be a witness against you and will eat your flesh like fire. You have heaped up treasure in the last days (James 5:1-3).

Verse one starts differently from the first three chapters. Instead of "my brethren" James addresses a different group, "you rich." Even though they appear to be blessed and set up for retirement, James announces that they've missed something. When they unwrap their retirement package someday they will be shocked to find nothing but misery! That's why the chapter opens with a command to "weep," and a participle to "keep on howling." These rich individuals can't understand how they've created for themselves misery. But the truth is that they are near the top of the misery index.

The motive underlying this section is covetousness. Covetousness is a superstitious attitude toward money and things that instinctively associates them with happiness. It's a mind-set, an inner dialog, that automatically connects money or things with an exciting life. It's like the lottery syndrome. Why play the lottery? One's chances of winning are zilch. But there is that remotest of remote possibility that one will win big, and be happy forever! And that infintesimal hope for happiness keeps one playing.

For example, several years ago, Eliberto Cantu of Lubbock, TX received a check for $177,000,00, his winnings in the Mega Millions lottery.[32] His response? "All I can say is, we're blessed – and keep buying lottery tickets!" That's the attitude of covetousness – big bucks blesses. "We are blessed" he said. James says, "no you aren't; you are cursed!" "And you might as well begin weeping and howling right now over your coming miseries."

Probably ninety percent of the world thinks that Eliberto Cantu has the rest of his life set up. He is on happiness street! And they're jealous, wishing it had happened to them. Covetousness instinctively associates one hundred seventy seven million dollars with happiness. James says, "absolutely not!"

The word "rich" fits much of the United States. Those of us who are above the poverty line in America are probably wealthier than ninety percent of the rest of the world. We are rich. This means we don't have to worry about things like where to get our next meal, or how soon we might lose our house and property, or whether we might get attacked or raped by the police. Those kinds of problems don't hound us like they do much of the world.

Think of Christians in Egypt. Several years ago, one of their churches was bombed and twenty eight attenders lost their lives. Within three months two more churches were bombed, one by a guy sitting on the front row of the church.[33] Think of how those events would change your perspective on Sunday morning worship attendance. Do you even think about a bomber sitting in the front seat of the sanctuary when you enter? No, we live in a much more secure environment, with a different set of expectations. We don't worry about terrorists; we don't worry about whether we are going to eat. We're rich.

Logan Pearsall Smith said, "to suppose as we all suppose, that we could be rich and not behave as the rich behave, is like supposing that we could drink whiskey all day long and stay sober."[34] Smith is saying that the common effect of living in a rich nation is a change in your inner dialog. Covetousness invades. That's what James is addressing. That's why we need this passage. Our society is pressuring us, whether we believe it or not. Jesus talked about the "deceitfulness of riches," like assuming that you can be rich as we are and stay sober.

James is so positive that misery is coming to these people that he commands them to begin weeping now. It's not "weep if you see these miseries coming," it's "weep now because they're on their way." Why?

I. Riches change one's thinking

Riches have a drawing power like strong magnets. You can't get near money and riches without feeling the pull to collect it and store it. The truth is that money doesn't stay with you. It flees, runs, slips, leaks, fizzles, decays, disappears. But people don't recognize that, especially when money captures their hearts and assures them that it's the key to their future bliss. They forget the verse that says, "Will you set your eyes on that which is not? For riches certainly make themselves wings; They fly away like an eagle toward heaven" (Proverbs 23:5). Setting your eyes on riches is setting your eyes on *that which is not.*

And money has changed the values of these rich: "*Your riches are corrupted, and your garments are moth-eaten. Your gold and silver are corroded, and their corrosion will be a witness against you and will eat your flesh like fire. You have heaped up treasure in the last days*" (*James 5:2-3*).

Covetousness turned them into collectors of garments and gold and silver and treasure. They probably rented multiple storage units. William Barclay records that there were three main sources of wealth in the east, and James chooses a word for the decay of each.[35]

There was *corn and grain*. That's the word, *corrupted, rotted*. Another form of wealth was *garments,* which James describes as *moth-eaten*. A third form was *gold and silver* which James says has *corroded*. We know that gold doesn't corrode. We also know that the clothes of wealthy people like us don't often get moth eaten. We take care of them. But James uses these metaphors to warn that resources which are stashed away for the future, disappear. God gives them to us *to use for others*. Once we set out to stash and store stuff a process begins:

A. Stored stuff decays. There are semi-legitimate reasons why people become collectors. Some came out of the depression where they had nothing and they want to make sure that never happens again. Others expect the apocalypse soon. But the basic reason why people rent storage spaces is because they don't understand that stuff can't stay in storage. Something happens inside the bin that reduces the value.

B. Decaying stuff *testifies* against you. The very presence of rust says, *it's not being used;* it's being stashed. Someday we will be judged by the amount of corrosion in our stuff. If you can't use it, find someone who can, because *that's its purpose on earth* — to be used!

C. Decaying stuff *eats your flesh*. Verse 3 describes their corrosive power as able to *eat your flesh like fire*. It attacks our bodies by adding to our worries about where to store it, how to protect it, what the stock market is doing, how many security devices we need.

Have your riches ever put you there? You don't own your stuff. It owns you. It scares you with what could happen, or does happen. It interrupts your schedule. It awakens you at night worrying about whether the suction noise you think you hear is your money down a tube. The point? You cannot successfully store your wealth for very long. It needs to be used.

II. Riches attack faith

By using the word faith in this title, I'm assuming that these rich were believers. What makes me think they have any faith? One of the clues is the word *heaped up* in verse 3, which also appears in Luke 12:21 *"So is he who lays up treasure for himself, and is not rich toward God."* *Lays up* is the same verb as *heaped up*.

Luke 12 tells the story of a rich fool who was pleasantly surprised by an abundant income. He didn't know what to do with it, but quickly came to a couple of conclusions: (a) that it belonged to him, (b) he could do with it what he wanted, and (c) he would store it.

So he said to himself, *"I will do this: I will pull down my barns and build greater, and there I will store all my crops and my goods. And I will say to my soul, 'Soul, you have many goods laid up for many years; take your ease; eat, drink, and be merry'"* *(Luke 12:18-19).*

He concluded that the purpose of his increased income was to store it for himself. Why store it? Because *he couldn't trust God with his future.* He was worried about his retirement portfolio. He had read the literature that said he needed to collect a million bucks to live successfully in retirement, and his new barns represented his money market investments. That's why he said, "Soul, you have many goods laid up for many years; take your ease; eat drink and be merry." His retirement was finally set.

But God said, *Fool!* Why ask where to store his crops? Couldn't he hear the cries of the needy all around him? Didn't he understand that his extra crops were from God to be used for others who were having trouble in their retirement years? Didn't he know that the God who had met his present needs with an abundance could also meet his retirement needs? How foolish. His bumper crop of blessing couldn't teach him about the faithfulness of God.

We need to think God's way about our retirement, because we live in a generation that believes this fool in Luke 12 was a smart investor! People around us will recommend we become like him. What that kind of thinking misses is in the phrase, "and is not rich toward God" (v. 21). Today we are being granted the opportunity to be rich toward God. Let's not miss it! America has the resources to evangelize the world if Christians would only buy up their opportunities to be rich toward God.

What we do with God's blessings is an issue of faith. We trust Him for the future by giving away our God-given assets to those in need. After all, He is the same "yesterday, today, and forever" (Hebrews 13:8). What He blessed us with today He can bless us with tomorrow.

III. Riches blind one to the urgency of the hour

"You have heaped up treasure in the last days" (v. 3). Messiah's return is near. The cut-off date is approaching quickly. But people were worrying about their IRAs and portfolios, like a man counting his twenty year collection of baseball cards while his house burns around him.

Jesus described this short-sighted attitude:

> But if that servant says in his heart, "My master is delaying his coming," and begins to beat the male and female servants, and to eat and drink and be drunk, the master of that servant will come on a day when he is not looking for him, and at an hour when he is not aware, and will cut him in two and appoint him his portion with the unbelievers. And that servant who knew his master's will,

and did not prepare himself or do according to his will, shall be beaten with many stripes (Luke 12:45-47).

With confidence that his master's return was delayed, the servant acted as if everything now belonged to him. In contrast, Jesus pictured the faithful servant this way:

> Who then is that faithful and wise steward, whom his master will make ruler over his household, to give them their portion of food in due season? Blessed is that servant whom his master will find so doing when he comes. Truly, I say to you that he will make him ruler over all that he has (Luke 12:42-44).

The difference between these two servants doesn't seem to be that one is a believer and the other is not. The difference shows up in their inner dialog. The one says in verse 45, "I don't have anything to worry about; I can do whatever I want to do." *And he missed his opportunity.* That's the way these rich people were thinking.

IV. Riches insulate one from the problems of the world

Indeed the wages of the laborers who mowed your fields, which you kept back by fraud, cry out; and the cries of the reapers have reached the ears of the Lord of Sabaoth. You have lived on the earth in pleasure and luxury; you have fattened your hearts as in a day of slaughter. You have condemned, you have murdered the just; he does not resist you (James 5:4-6).

Were these people actual believers, or were they unbelievers? The difference between "you rich" in verse 1 and "brethren" in 7 cause commentaries to argue over the spiritual condition of the rich. The interesting thing is that whatever position the writer takes, he or she almost always believes that the passage should be applied to us today. We, as believers, are rich, and perhaps this passage could be describing genuine Christians.

At any rate it should warn us. It pictures the end result of those who live for pleasure in 4:1-5, who swallow the world's superstition that money is life, money is god, and we have to grab for all the gusto we can get. The result is "being spotted by the world" (1:27). Maybe that's why James leaves the picture unspecified. They could be believers. On the other hand, they might not be. It's hard to tell.

What is clear is how the thirst for wealth has changed these people. It has changed their attitudes toward their brothers and sisters. They've become like Cain, asking, "am I my brother's keeper?"

At the same time their success doesn't look exactly legal. For example, they haven't paid their laborers in verse 4, they've lived in luxury and "murdered the just" in verses 5 and 6. Their empathy for others who don't enjoy their success seems to have hardened.

A. They became blind to their opportunities to help the needy. Even their own laborers who mowed their lawns, escaped their glance. They had a great chance to become rich toward God by blessing them. But somehow they missed the opportunity because they were busy with other things.

B. They weren't even paying their employees. Apparently the laborers had no legal way of getting their rightful wages, and the rich simply ignored them. After all they were only laborers or temporary reapers. They weren't important enough to bother with. Covetousness blinded them to their responsibility. When covetousness sets in, the value of other people changes. We saw this attitude in chapter 2 when the usher didn't understand that every person in the body was important. But here it looks like the poor have slipped even further in the hearts of these rich, almost to the realm of complete insignificance.

C. They condemned the one they should have received. James is perhaps thinking of Judas, who traded away the most precious person on earth for thirty pieces of silver (John 12:6, Matthew 26:14-16). What a deal! What an idiot! An example of massively misplaced values. Judas was covetous. And "he said this, not because he cared about the poor . . ." (John 12:6). That's where these rich were, disciples of Judas.

The magnet of money can so transform a person that he will condemn and murder, in the sense of running over the righteous. A righteous person is special in God's sight. But covetousness encourages one to see a righteous individual as an easier target to exploit because he won't resist.

V. Their money fueled their desires

Like the rich fool in Luke 12:17 who wondered what to do with all his new income, they choose to invest it on bigger barns. After all if you have money to buy a Rolls Royce, why buy a Chevy?

James says, *"you have lived on the earth in pleasure and luxury; you have fattened your hearts as in a day of slaughter"* (James 5:5).

They fattened their hearts in the same way farmers fatten cows for slaughter, by making couch-potato cows out of them. Riches turn people into fat cows. Christians can get out of shape not only physically, but spiritually, and morally. That kind of fat-cow living sets one up for the day of slaughter, when God judges. God's judgment is even described as a day of slaughter (Jeremiah 12:3; 7:32, 19:6).

J. A. Motyer says, "it's as if James is saying, 'oh to be a thin beast the day the butcher comes!' Such a beast is safe. The slaughterman has no wish to count ribs!"[36]

The bottom line is that *covetousness sidetracks us from real life*. It encourages us to waste our time and energy on nothingness. Jack Whittaker, for example, won more than one hundred million dollars in a Powerball jackpot in December 2002. But then he had to figure out how to keep it safe, and how to deal with beggars looking for a handout, and how much to give to the people he wanted to help.

So he bought his sixteen year old granddaughter a new car and she turned to drugs. Within two years both his granddaughter and her boyfriend were dead from drug overdoses.

He was plagued with beggar requests. He was robbed of a half million dollars. He's been in and out of court, even in and out of jail, all because the money distracted him from real living. "I wish I'd torn that ticket up," he sobbed to reporters at the time of his granddaughter's death.[37] What happened? He *thought he had been blessed!* He didn't understand the truth of James that he had been cursed and should have started sobbing as soon as he received the check. The lesson? *Covetousness sucks happiness from life. It wastes life.* Our job is **life.** Build wisely. It is the only real thing you will ever build.

We are building for eternity. Don't let money, things, retirement, distract you from your job. You only get to do it once. And then you live for eternity in what you constructed. Paul declares:

> therefore we make it our aim, whether present or absent, to be well pleasing to Him. For we must all appear before the judgment seat of Christ, that each one may receive the things done in the body, according to what he has done, whether good or bad (2 Corinthians 5:9-10).

How can we fight against the pervasively covetous influence of our culture? I have found valuable guidance in 1 Timothy 6. Here are some suggestions:

1. Start with contentment. *"Now godliness with contentment is great gain. For we brought nothing into this world, and it is certain we can carry nothing out. And having food and clothing, with these we shall be content" (1 Timothy 6:6-8).*

Surveys among high-income earners show us that no matter how high their incomes, they need at least fifty percent more income to be happy. No amount will ever be enough until you can learn to be happy with what you currently earn. What do you need to make you content right now? Lack of contentment suggests that you are covetous. J. Brotherton said, "my riches consist not in the extent of my possessions but in the fewness of my wants."[38]

2. Fight against your attraction to money and things. *"But those who desire to be rich fall into temptation and a snare, and into many foolish and harmful lusts which drown men in destruction and perdition. For the love of money is a root of all kinds of evil, for which some have strayed from the faith in their greediness, and pierced themselves through with many sorrows" (1 Timothy 6:9-10).*

Joe E. Lewis once said, "it doesn't matter if you're rich or poor, as long as you've got money."[39] But *it does matter.* Lewis' obvious joke is Paul's exact point, that the passion for money changes you. It's not how much, it's not how rich or poor one is, it's how *attractive* it is. Beggars can pierce themselves with many sorrows by their love of money.

3. Don't trust money to give you life. *"Command those who are rich in this present age not to be haughty, nor to trust in uncertain riches but in the living God, who gives us richly all things to enjoy" (1 Timothy 6:17).*

Notice Paul doesn't say "they're wrong for being rich." He doesn't say, "tell them to get rid of their riches." The danger is getting within the magnetic sphere of wealth and getting sucked into thinking that there's some hope there. Instead, our hope is in the "living God who gives us richly all things to enjoy!" God is the only One who can bring joy. Money has a dismal track record of supplying anything more than misery.

And surprisingly, He wants to give us "richly all things to enjoy." What an incredible statement! God wants to give us *all things to enjoy!* And He wants to do it *richly!* What an amazing God!

4. Learn to trust God with your needs. How do we trust God? *"Let them do good, that they be rich in good works, ready to give, willing to share, storing up for themselves a good foundation for the time to come, that they may lay hold on eternal life" (1 Timothy 6:18-19).*

The truth is that when we have money in our hands we *don't have the real thing.* We think we are rich but it's fake. However, we can use that money as trade bait, and exchange it for eternal things. How? Verse 18 says, "by doing good, by being rich in good works, by being ready to give and willing to share." That's the way to invest in the eternal stock market which pays dividends forever!

"There is one who makes himself rich, yet *has* nothing; *And* one who makes himself poor, yet *has* great riches" (Proverbs 13:7). Which are you? Should you weep and howl? Or rejoice?

Chapter 14

The Challenge of Waiting
(and the deception that thinks it might be better to quit)

James 5:7-12

It's one thing to be a lottery winner. It's a much different thing to be a promise holder. Verses 1-6 address the lottery winners. But verses 7-12 speak to the promise holders as if they are the real lottery winners. The promise is of precious fruit (v. 7) in contrast to the "misery" in the previous section.

The rich had "heaped up treasure" (v. 3) because they were already in possession of life's valuables. All they had to do was stash it somewhere. In contrast, those with God's promise weren't seeing anything that looked like treasure, and perhaps wondered as they caught a glimpse of the rich whether their promise was worth waiting for. The contrast isn't between the rich and poor, but between the covetous whose money is their god and those who by faith are obeying the Word.

Maybe that's why James contrasts you rich and brethren. The you rich may be brothers also, but not the kind James admired because they were laying up treasure on earth. The brethren were obeying God's Word even though they couldn't see much happening. James assures them, "you will love the outcome; just wait until the Lord reveals Himself!" (v. 11).

"Be patient" is the challenge. The command appears in verses 7, 8, 10, and 11. That's the key not only to this section but one of the underlying themes in the book. "Don't quit. Don't give up. Don't stop living for Jesus Christ by doing the Word, even though it seems like nothing is coming from all you've invested." The idea of patience appears eight times in this passage using four different Greek words. I've highlighted them in this quote:

> Therefore **be patient**, brethren, until the coming of the Lord. See how the farmer **waits** for the precious fruit of the earth, waiting **patiently** for it until it receives the early and latter rain. You also **be patient**. Establish your hearts, for the coming of the Lord is at hand. Do not grumble against one another, brethren, lest you be condemned. Behold, the Judge is standing at the door! My brethren, take the prophets, who spoke in the name of the Lord, as an example of **suffering** and **patience.** Indeed we count them blessed who **endure.** You have heard of the **perseverance** of Job and seen the end intended by the Lord -- that the Lord is very compassionate and merciful. But above all, my brethren, do not swear, either by heaven or by earth or with any other oath. But let your "Yes," be "Yes," and your "No," "No," lest you fall into judgment (James 4:7-12).

Patience appears three times in verse 7. "Be patient" is the Greek word, *makrothumeo*, which means "don't lose heart, don't give up." "The farmer waits" is *ekdeckomai*, which means "to wait expectantly in anticipation." Then "waiting patiently" is the word *makrothumeo* again. Verse 8 has *makrothumeo* a third time, "be patient." Verse 10 has "suffering" *kakopatheia*, which adds the ideas *evil* and *emotional* to the difficult situation. And the word, "patience" is *makrothumia* again, this time the noun. Verse 11 uses the word, "endure," twice, once as a verb and once as a noun, "perseverance." Both are the Greek word, *hupomeno*, which means, "to stay under when it gets hot, to stand firm, no matter what happens."

These four Greek words summarize the thrust of James' letter to the twelve tribes which were scattered (1:1). Back at the start he instructed them to "count it all joy" knowing that the testing of their faith will produce "patience" (1:3). The word "produces" means "to accomplish, achieve, bring about." Various trials *test* our faith and *bring about patience.* That same word *patience* appears here twice in 5:11.

The striking thing is that back in 1:4 James declares that it's this process of *trials working patience* that makes us "perfect and complete, lacking nothing." Perfection and completeness, meaning *maturity and holiness* were the ultimate goals James had for writing this little letter. Even though the readers were under stress because of the scattering, James knew that God was powerful enough to use the worst of trials to bring about their maturity and holiness.

All along James has had this thought of patience in the back of his mind. He talked about how their stress might encourage someone to speak unwisely to and about others (2:1-13; 3:9-12, 14-16; 4:11-12), or quit and live for pleasure (4:1-6; 5:1-6), or become a hypocrite by talking without doing (2:14-26; 4:13-17). Each of those situations was a patience/endurance issue.

And patience is not simply waiting. It *is* waiting, but it's waiting in spite of the difficulties, in spite of the lack of hope, in spite of the fact that waiting doesn't seem to be worth the effort. It's waiting when the situation calls for quitting. It's waiting when all your perseverance has seemed to fail.

We think of patience when a person is being burned at the stake, or trying to live for Christ under threat of death. But it also involves saying *no* to pornography, and living for Christ in a family that ridicules you, or at a job where you are treated as trash. Patience is needed to raise children in today's pressures, to remain faithfully serving in a church where your efforts are not appreciated or noticed.

James is saying in the worst of these situations – ***Don't quit!*** The best is yet to come!

He develops this command to be patient by answering two of the major questions that arise: *why?* And *how?*

I. Why continue to wait?

James gives four motivating reasons why we should keep going:

A. The fruit is not quite ripe. "*See how the farmer waits for the precious fruit of the earth, waiting patiently for it until it receives the early and latter rain*" (v. 7).

Patience involves thinking like a farmer. Some things can't be sped up. There's nothing a farmer can do to make his crops produce faster. There are no instant fertilizers that can produce fruit in half the time. He has to wait for it to mature.

Jewish farmers knew that raising crops took an early and a latter rain. Fruit was not ready to pick after the early rain, which normally arrived in October or November. The later rains didn't arrive for four or five more months, in April and May.

What kind of patience did the farmer need? Was he enduring persecution? Was he waiting until the end of his life? No, he was waiting for circumstances and the climate to take its necessary and familiar course. The hardships he may have suffered in the process were those of everyday life. In a similar way, the readers were facing the repeated difficulties of daily human life, enhanced as we have seen by their refugee status, and needed to view them through a farmer's eyes. Farming teaches that *fruit takes time*.

William Barclay tells us that the word for *don't give up*, *makrothumeo*, only appears in the Bible. It doesn't appear in classical Greek and only a few times in later Greek, because the Greeks apparently had no patience for patience! They saw no virtue in it.

But in the Bible the word has two basic uses. First it means *a steadfast spirit that will never give in.*[40] It was because Abraham *patiently endured* that he received the promise (Hebrews 6:15). It's the patience of the prophets who never gave up their hope in God no matter how painful their lives became. It's a patience that says, "God's Word is true, I can trust it with everything I have, and I am going to keep doing that very thing."

The second use builds on the first. It's a patient attitude *toward others*; it's a spirit that might take revenge if it chose, but refuses the thought. It never retaliates. The Greeks had a substitute *virtue* for this. It was the word, *megalopsuchia*, which Aristotle defined as the refusal to tolerate any insult or injury. For a Greek, it was right to go all out for vengeance! That may be why they never used the word, *makrothumia.*[41]

James employs both of these definitions in this passage. The eight times James uses synonyms for patience are all used in the sense of the first definition, *don't give up*. But the second definition fits the thought of verses 9 and 12, the two verses that seem to jar the thought. What do *grumbling* and *swearing* have to do with patience? Verse 9 says, "Do not grumble against one another." That's patience, a steadfast spirit that will never give in, *no matter what brothers and sisters do*. And when verse 12 commands, "do not swear," James again has in mind our patient reactions *with one another.*

The point is that you and I are like farmers. We plant seeds expecting to reap fruit. We plant by the things we do and say. We sow seeds of encouragement, correction, joy, peace, carefulness by our responses. Those seeds are going to bear fruit. You may wonder why *days to harvest* is taking longer than expected and you can't shorten the fruit production process. But the Creator designed it that way.

B. The Lord is at hand. Why quit the day before Christ comes back? Why give up one hundred yards before the finish line? *The*

Lord is at hand means that the time is very short, in spite of the feeling that it might take forever. Prophetic events on the calendar are much closer than we think.

Farmers are motivated by the harvest. When Christ returns, *we will see the harvest.* Scripture writers keep encouraging us that it's coming. Paul said, "Therefore, my beloved brethren, be steadfast, immovable, always abounding in the work of the Lord, knowing that your labor is not in vain in the Lord" (1 Corinthians 15:58).

We attend the funerals of people close to us, we hear the news that someone else has been given six months to live. The truth is that our Lord may be back tonight. The Lord is near, right at the door. We may hear the knock at any moment. I spoke recently to a good friend who is ninety four years old. When I asked him what he was doing he said, "I'm sitting here waiting for my call!"

C. Our Lord has yet to reveal His incredible beauty. *"You have heard of the perseverance of Job and seen the end intended by the Lord — that the Lord is very compassionate and merciful" (v. 11).*

I probably should have entitled this section, "you ain't seen nothin yet!" "Wait till you see how our Lord adds it all up!" His beauty is shown in these two marvelous words, *compassionate* and *merciful.* Compassion means that from the deepest parts of God's inner being come love and affection. It's love and affection that don't depend on the other person.[42]

Think of the Good Samaritan. A Jewish man on his way down to Jericho was robbed, beaten and left for dead. In his state he had no ability to call or influence anyone. He just lay on the side of the road. This meant that any positive response had to come from the person passing by.

The priest and the Levite didn't respond, which revealed their lack of compassion for a brother. Nothing in their religion compelled them to stop. The Samaritan approached as an enemy, a visitor to the area, probably in a hurry to get in and out since Jewish people did not treat Samaritans kindly. But Luke 10:33 says that he "had compassion." Something in his nature was merciful and kind. James uses the same word here, adding a prefix to emphasize *all* or *full of* compassion.

The word *merciful* speaks of His sympathy, and generosity, forgiveness, His sharing in our difficulty and grief. Have you ever pictured God as full of affection? Full of sympathy? Desirous of sharing our difficulty and grief? That's probably what John 3:16 has in mind with *for God so loved the world.*

The verse says, "you have heard of the perseverance of Job." Perhaps you wouldn't think of Job as one who had *perseverance.* Even though he started well and worshiped God in chapter 1 when he lost everything, and didn't sin in chapter 2 when his wife encouraged him to "curse God and die," things didn't go as well when his three friends showed up.

Job wasn't burned at the stake; for him it was living another day with pain. He wasn't crucified on a cross; he was only talking with three friends who were convinced he was a big sinner. He was not persecuted for his faith, except at the hands of his well-meaning friends. His wounds came from friendly fire.

Job didn't see God's compassion and mercy until the *end.* He didn't see it in chapter 3 when he cursed the day of his birth (3:1), or in chapter 6 when he said that God was shooting poisoned arrows at him (6:4). He didn't see God's intended purpose in chapter 9 when he said, "Even if I summoned him and he responded, I do not believe he would give me a hearing. He would crush me with a storm and multiply my wounds for no reason. He would not let me regain my breath but would overwhelm me with misery" (Job 9:16-18).

That statement doesn't sound very positive. Yet that's Job, who is persevering. That's not nice language when speaking of God. Have you ever felt that way? Do you think that Job would have said at that time, "I am speaking to One who is very compassionate and merciful?" No, he hadn't yet met Him in that way.

Have you ever wanted to say that kind of thing? How could a person like Job, with this much pent-up anger against God ever change? Simple. He met God. It began in chapter 38, after about thirty chapters of painful discussion. Up until that time there wasn't much that Job saw of compassion and mercy. But in the end he found that God was very compassionate and merciful. Job's words in the last chapter are, "I have heard of You by the hearing of the ear, But now my eye sees You" (Job 42:5).

Notice that Job only met God in and through the difficulty. Suppose he had given up and quit after chapter 9, or 16? Suppose he had kicked his friends out and obeyed his wife, and cursed God and died? He would have never met God in all His compassion and mercy. That doesn't mean he would have gone to hell. Rather it means that he would have missed the joy and peace, the *blessing* God had designed for him. God showed the depths of His compassion and mercy to Job because he didn't *quit*. It was Job's patient endurance that allowed the fruit to ripen. In a similar way God wants to bless us by revealing Himself to us, which *He can only do through the process of difficulty.*

Notice also that God had this goal in mind for Job from the beginning. It's in the phrase, "the end intended by the Lord." From the start, when God allowed Satan to touch Job and bring in the painful disasters, and then again afflict Job with an awful disease, God had a purpose, a goal. It wasn't just an accident, it wasn't a weak escape from what would have been a bad ending. *It was designed.* Satan said, "I'll take it all away so he will curse you." And God said, "no, I'll use it to double bless him!"

James wants his readers to know that God is saying the same thing about their trials: *God will use them to double bless you!* Remember these were people whose lives had turned for the worse after they trusted Christ. They were scattered because of their faith. They refugees without jobs, homes, or land. If they quit now, *they might never get to meet on earth the God of all compassion and mercy!*

D. Those who endure are blessed. *"Indeed we count them blessed who endure"* (v. 11). The word "indeed" is the word, "see," "behold," or "look." It's a word that asks us to stop and evaluate who the people are that are genuinely blessed. Movie stars? Lottery winners? Thieves? Powerful people in high places?

James said, "blessed is the man who endures temptation" (1:12), and "this one will be blessed in what he does" (1:25). Soren Kierkegaard said most of us are like the schoolboy who stole his teacher's answer sheet before a math exam. His aim was to memorize the answers for each of the problems, score a 100% on the exam, and get an "A" in the course. But answers acquired that way are no answers at all, except in a technical sense. "To truly have the answers," said Kierkegaard, "we must first work through the problems."[43]

Imagine getting this note:

> To Whom It May Concern:
>
> I hate my life. You can't imagine the ache of wanting to end your life and not being able to because you're a quadriplegic and can't use your hands.
> After the doctors did surgery on my neck, I refused to wear a neck collar. I hate it too. Nobody understands, and nobody will listen to me when I tell them I don't want to live. People feel sorry for me, and I can't stand it. I can't even go to the bathroom by myself.
> I don't have the energy to cope. I don't have the strength to face the next day. I want out.
> A depressed teen

What would you say to this teen? I'm sure you would want to help her. Would the directions James gives here be of any help, or would you suggest she consider ending her life prematurely? What hope is there for someone who is a permanent quadriplegic?

The truth is that James gives exactly what this young girl needs: "don't quit because the fruit is not ripe yet;" "don't quit because the Lord is at hand;" "don't quit because you have yet to see His incredible beauty;" and "don't quit because those who endure are blessed."

The rest of the story is that the depressed teen did not quit and now, more than 50 years later still demonstrates in her life the incredible beauty of the Lord and His incredible blessing on her. She is Joni Eareckson Tada.[44]

II. How can one find the strength to wait?

James gives four commands to help us understand *how* to stand strong in the pain: *establish your hearts* (8), *don't grumble* (9), *take the prophets as your example* (10), and *don't swear* (12). These four commands explain the attitudes that God responds to.

A. Strengthen YOUR Heart. *"You also be patient. Establish your hearts, for the coming of the Lord is at hand" (v. 8).*

Establish means, "to strengthen, make firm, set" our hearts. It's similar to what we do physically, we strengthen the heart muscle with exercise. To run in an Iron man race, a person needs a heart that can beat one hundred eighty beats a minute for ten hours. Apart from that strength, a person is not ready for the Iron man. Where does one get this kind of strength? Exercise.

But there is another kind of heart in the Iron man. It's displayed by people who are worn out at the end of a grueling race and collapse, but don't quit. They *crawl* to the finish line. That's *heart*. That's the kind of heart James has in mind. Where does it come from? It's largely how you *talk to yourself*.

The distance runner trains by talking himself or herself into another inch, another block, another mile, another ten miles, a faster time. He's convincing his body that he can do what he says he can do, so that on the day of the race when he says, "I'm going to make that finish line," his body responds. You strengthen it by repeating the truth.

Steve Fluet, who has completed twelve Ironman races said this:

> "My last one was incredible in terms of showing me how mental these races are. I crashed at mile fifty two and really did some damage to my body (major road rash). After a long time on the ground I was able to get up and continue and finish the race with my second fastest IM race time. Yes it hurt, especially on the running part (twenty six miles, remember). The pain was awful, but I was able to focus so much more mentally to allow myself to get through the run."[45]

In a similar way, **we strengthen our hearts by faith,** by what we believe, what we repeatedly practice saying to ourselves. James has mentioned four truths he wants us to believe and preach to ourselves: (a) the fruit is not ripe; God is not finished with me (b) the Lord will be back in a few minutes; why quit now? (c) you haven't seen the beauty of the Lord's compassion and mercy; (d) we count them blessed who endure.

B. Strengthen others. *"Do not grumble against one another, brethren, lest you be condemned. Behold, the Judge is standing at the door!" (v. 9).*

The word *grumble* means "to groan against someone else." It's a strong word, an emphatic expression of discontentment. It's not only dissatisfaction with a person, but also with God. It's not just criticism, complaining, sighing, but criticism that *attacks the entire project.*

One person's loud discontentment can weaken the entire group. It invites judgment from the Lord, because the person grumbled

against is His child, has been predestined to become holy and
without blame, and is a valuable part of Christ's body. The grumbler
is going after God's arrangement and God's people. The threat is
"lest you be condemned."

Condemned for what? Cutting off what God has put together.
It's similar to your physical body. What condemnation will you
receive by cutting off your arm? You will suffer for the rest of your
life. God has put you in a spiritual body, the body of Christ. What
condemnation will you receive by cutting off a brother or sister who
may be the arm of the body? You will suffer the rest of your life.

C. Study success stories. *"My brethren, take the prophets, who spoke
in the name of the Lord, as an example of suffering and patience. Indeed we count
them blessed who endure" (vv. 10-11).*

Encouragement comes by reviewing stories of the prophets.
Take, for example, the time when Elijah wanted to quit. He heard the
news that old queen Jezebel had threatened to kill him. He had just
brought the nation of Israel to a decision point of serving Jehovah
instead of serving Baal on mount Carmel, he had just killed four
hundred fifty of her Baal-worshiping prophets, had just prayed in
rain for the first time in three and a half years, and now he hears that
Jezebel wanted his head, off of his body. What did he do? He ran like
a scared deer, all the way down to Beersheba and laid down under a
juniper tree and cried to the Lord to let him die (1 Kings 18-19).

God's answer? *It's too early for you to die!* "Don't you think that the
One who kept the rain away for three and a half years, who answered
your prayers so spectacularly on mount Carmel and burned up the
soaking wet sacrifice, can take care of Jezebel? What's your problem?
If I allow you to leave earth at this moment, you are going to miss
too much. You are not alone because I still have seven thousand
people who haven't bowed the knee to Baal (1 Kings 19:13-18).
Besides I have an ending planned for your life that no one else has

ever experienced or seen, a trip into eternity on a chariot of fire! It's too early to quit. So get up and obey."

Indeed we count them blessed who endure. Do we count them blessed enough to want to be part of their number? How do we *count* them? Do we admire them? Do we long to be like them and imitate their behavior? The truth of the matter is that *what God has done in their lives, He can do and wants to do in our lives.* Our circumstances will be different, but God's infinite compassion and mercy is the same today.

D. Speak truth. *"But above all, my brethren, do not swear, either by heaven or by earth or with any other oath. But let your 'Yes,' be 'Yes,' and your 'No,' 'No,' lest you fall into judgment"* (v. 12).

James is not talking about cussing, but making an oath which guarantees that what you are now going to say is the truth: "I swear to God;" "I swear on a stack of Bibles;" "I promise, promise, promise, cross my heart and hope to die."

Swearing is an attempt to guarantee that certain words are true. And Christ's response is, "no, make every word true; let your yes actually mean total yes, and your no mean really no." Christ added, "anything beyond absolute truth comes from the evil one" (Matthew 5:37).

Any time you have to *swear* that something is true suggests the presence of words you say which are not true. You swear because you have accepted the theology that you don't *always* have to tell the truth. There are times when a little embellishment livens up the conversation.

James says, "no, you can't speak honestly with yourself if you are not speaking honestly with others. And you can't strengthen your heart when you are lying to yourself." Genuine spiritual exercise only comes from telling your heart the truth. *Liars do not endure difficult times.* They quit because their rhetorically created fantasy world crumbles.

What kind of truth do you speak to your heart? The same four facts that James has already emphasized – the fruit is not ready yet, wait a little; the Lord is at hand, it won't be long; He is going to reveal compassion and mercy that you can't believe; and God's blessing is for those who endure.

What can we learn from this section?

1. Don't quit. The best is yet to come. Think of Job and the *end* intended by our compassionate Lord. Memorize God's Word. Spend time with other believers. Keep in church.

2. Realize that you may be the reason for someone else's endurance. You may say the encouraging word to someone ready to give it up. Think of what others are going through and encourage them.

3. Live in gratefulness for what God has done for you. Remember the former days and the incredible blessing of salvation in Christ. Paul never forgot that. He says in 2 Corinthians 4:1, "Having received mercy, we faint not."

4. Confess and embarrass yourself every time you catch yourself embellishing the truth, or lying. Don't tolerate any falsehood.

Chapter 15

The Challenge of Prayer
(and the deception that assumes no one is listening)

James 5:13-20

Everyone knows that prayer is valuable. The question is "how valuable?" Valuable enough to invest extra time? Valuable enough to quit other things in order to pray? It's not that we are against prayer. The question is, "how much is enough?"

In this last section of James continues answering the question he brought up in 7-12, the question, "how?" This could be the fifth command in James' explanation of how to keep walking with God when nothing is happening. In addition to *strengthen your hearts* (v. 8), and *don't grumble* (v. 9), and *take the prophets for an example* (v. 10), and *don't swear* (v. 12), this section adds, *pray in every circumstance of life*. These circumstances include, *difficulties* and *blessings* (v. 13), *sickness* (vv. 14-16a), *sin* (v. 16), *national sin* (vv. 16b-18), and *family problems* (vv. 19-20).

I. Life's situations call for prayer

The word *pray* appears seven times in this section. There are things we can do *after* we pray, but there is not much we can do *until* we pray. God has designed all of our life to lead us to Him in prayer.

A. The answer to difficulties is prayer. *"Is anyone among you suffering? Let him pray" (v. 13).* The word *suffering* is the word *trouble.* It's a word that refers to evil blows that come from the outside. It's when life doesn't work right, isn't fair, doesn't include you, doesn't meet your desires and expectations. You suffer. It gets to you; you're frustrated, emotional, discouraged, beaten down, tired.

Let him pray means that God always wants us to turn to Him so that He can demonstrate His ability in the situation. God often introduces Himself to us in the middle of trouble, if we will pray. Trouble may come in thousands of different forms, but the answer is always the same, simply *pray.* There is no promise that God will transform a situation without prayer.

Have you experienced God answering *your* prayer? It is possible to live for years with a casual relationship with God, that doesn't talk about anything very seriously. But something special happens when we see Him working out our problems. Maybe things remain unfinished in our lives because we haven't turned to God in prayer

B. The response to blessings is prayer. *"Is anyone cheerful? Let him sing psalms" (v. 13).* The word, *cheerful* is a combination of the word *well* and *soul.* It's someone who is experiencing the *good life,* someone who feels alive. It's talking about a deep inner sense of peace and well-being.

The command to *sing psalms* may be a little fuzzy to us. The word originally meant to *twang a string with your hands,* or *play a stringed instrument.*[46] Get your guitar or harp out and start strumming. Make noise, music. Later on the word developed to include all types of music and singing and praise. But the point is when God has given you an honest reason to be happy, then praise God, *out loud,* so others can hear. It means to praise the Lord in a musical expression, whether you sing or blow a horn or twang a string.

You can praise God quietly, but this is the kind of praise where you say something. You want others to know what God has done and be encouraged. Praise is the kind of good news that travels fast. Gossip control enjoys sending out questions like, "did you hear the way God protected _____ in that accident?" "Did you hear the testimony of _____ when he stepped on the snake? God wants His people to be a singing and praising people, things that need to be done out loud.

The Bible repeatedly commands us to praise God out loud: "Oh give thanks to the LORD; call upon his name; make known his deeds among the peoples Sing to him; sing praises to him; tell of all his wondrous works" (1 Chronicles 16:8-9); Or "Oh come, let us sing to the LORD; let us make a joyful noise to the rock of our salvation Let us come into his presence with thanksgiving; let us make a joyful noise to him with songs of praise" (Psalm 95:1-2).

Think of the hundreds of blessings we have received. Have we made any corresponding notes of praise? We should greet everyone with "I have been greatly blessed, because my God is amazing."

II. Sickness calls for prayer

Is anyone among you sick? Let him call for the elders of the church, and let them pray over him, anointing him with oil in the name of the Lord. And the prayer of faith will save the sick, and the Lord will raise him up. And if he has committed sins, he will be forgiven. Confess your trespasses to one another, and pray for one another, that you may be healed (James 5:14-16a).

Faith healers get the headlines because they appear in the media with attractive programs and great assurances that they are the servants of God with the true power of the apostles.

But James doesn't recommend his readers look for someone with the gift of healing. He recommends the church, and the elders of the church. Why them? They may not have healed anyone in their lives. What do they know about healing?

The real question is not, "what do they know," but "Who do they know!" The issue is not their resume' but their faith, and their purity before the Lord.

A. God does heal – in response to prayer! How does it work? We had a lady at our church, a new believer, who was daily getting worse with Huntington's disease. She was in a women's Bible study on James, came upon this passage, called me and said, "do you guys do this?" I said, "yes, we believe and obey the Bible." She said, "will you come and pray for me?" I said, "sure." So we did, following the directions in this passage. James gives at least six directions here:

1. The sick person *requests* the church elders to come and pray. This is a decision made by the sick person – *let him call*. Elders are normal guys, not apostles or prophets. We had no healers among us as we drove to this woman's house that Tuesday evening, all six of us in the same car. I remember comments like, "I don't feel like a healer." "We don't have any special powers." We were just responding to a call for help, in Jesus' name.

It's important to realize that this passage does not encourage us to ignore doctors. If you come down with acute appendicitis at one am in the morning, don't call the elders to come and pray over you. Call your doctor or go to the Emergency room.

2. The elders *come* to the sick person. They can pray from a distance, but they need to go to the scene of the sickness, even if the sick one might have something catching. You can't anoint the sick person with oil by remote control. They need to enter the scene, see the suffering and interact with the sufferer. It's a pastoral situation; they enter the sick room to minister, to counsel, to encourage, to pray. How different from the razmataz of the faith healer, where you go to him and he bops you on the head. We are shepherds; which means we empathize and work with individual sheep.

3. The elders *anoint* the sick person with oil. Some think that this is medical oil, which is to be rubbed in. That would be like saying, "let the elders come and administer their medicine and pray for the healing." I question whether the oil is anything special. The cures do not stem from the properties of the oil, but from the power of the Lord to heal. The oil is symbolic. We are not coming with holy oil, or magic oil; we are not coming as healers with unusual powers; we are coming in obedience to God's directions, in our weak states, to help someone weaker than us, by *praying*. The oil simply symbolizes the task.

4. Then the elders are to *pray over him.* It doesn't say how long they are to pray, or what they are to pray about, although the context mentions sin. "And if he has committed sins, he will be forgiven." The cure comes from God in a context of humility and purity. This means that the sufferer needs to know that he or she is to confess sin. Perhaps the sickness is connected with sin. Or perhaps he or she remembers past sins that previously have been ignored. You wouldn't expect God to heal a person when the sickness has come as a judgment from God (as in 1 Corinthians 11:30). So the prayer should include the sin as well as the sickness.

When we went to the house of the woman with Huntingtons, we fasted all day, then gathered first at the church to pray and confess our sins to one another. We then went and prayed for the woman and left. Her husband had baked a cake for us, which we devoured, and then went to a local restaurant for a meal.

We didn't see anything unusual happen. We simply prayed, cleaned up the cake and left. But when the woman came to a Bible study at church the next day she announced that she had been healed. Her symptoms had all been arrested. It was exciting! I had never seen that kind of instant healing before, even though I had heard stories of it happening to others. She was actually parading around the women in the class, praising God and holding up objects in her hands, which she couldn't do before.

5. It's the *prayer* that saves the sick. This isn't a ministry of anointing, or even healing, but praying. It's not the oil, it's not the method, but the prayer and the cleansing that saves the sick. It's the prayer of faith, the prayer that believes and obeys the promises of God even if the elders feel weak and unqualified. They may acknowledge that they have never done this before and don't know what to do, but that doesn't matter. It's the prayer, the confession of sin, the trust in God that makes the difference.

6. The Lord will raise him up. The healing comes from God alone, nothing else. It's a simple request from a group of leaders about one of their friends who is suffering. They have no *clout* with God, no extra authority apart from their position as leaders of the church. All they do is ask in obedience to God's word.

How about the word *will*? It promises that the prayer of faith *will* save the sick." Isn't that a guarantee? Can we expect that such prayer will automatically save the sick person? He doesn't say, *might*, or *should,* or *maybe,* or even, *if God wills.* He says, *will.* Can we therefore expect full answers to our prayers? Will God always heal a sick person?

Faith healers camp on this verse. They say that this verse gives you permission to *demand* healing from the Lord. Oral Roberts used to pray on his radio programs, demanding God to heal the person whose hand was on the radio, "from the crown of his head, to the sole of his foot." It seemed to be done with the attitude, "You said you would do it, You promised, now do it; I command you." To me, that sounded a little arrogant. Where do we find that kind of praying in the Bible?

The answer is, "no, this is not a guarantee that God will heal every one." Not even in apostolic times, when the apostles had ability to heal many, did God heal everyone. But that doesn't mean that we aren't encouraged to ask in prayer.

What's so amazing here is that we can ask in faith for whatever we desire, and leave the results up to His wise response! There are people who want to be able to get what they desire from God. They want assurance that their request will automatically be answered. But if God obeyed our every request, we would have to quit praying because of our lack of wisdom as to what and how to ask. Think of some of the things you've asked for, which you now see to be ridiculous.

Ruth Bell Graham, Bill Graham's wife, said, "If God had answered every prayer of mine, I would have married the wrong man seven times."[47] There is so little we know about God's plan for our lives. I would never want to miss God's plan by commanding Him to do what I think best. Every request should be made in the spirit of *Thy will be done.*

III. Sin calls for prayer

Confess your trespasses to one another, and pray for one another, that you may be healed. The effective, fervent prayer of a righteous man avails much (James 5:16).

A. Sin is similar to sickness. It does things to our insides like sickness does to our bodies. For example: (1) *It gets worse if it is hidden and unattended.* How long do you have to ignore cancer before it is out of control? Sin becomes a monster over time. As we hide it, it becomes more and more powerful. (2) *It changes the balance of our lives.* Like sickness, it can interrupt all you are doing and put you down and out for days. (3) *It can ruin you and lead to death.* Think of the instant changes that take place when the doctor announces *cancer*. Cancer is not a friend. It doesn't enter your life to enrich you. Neither is pornography, or anger or lying. James is saying, "when we have sin around, things are not normal; we need healing."

B. The only cure starts with confession. How do you deal with sin? Hide it? Grit your teeth and determine to do better? Plead with God to help you turn over a new leaf? Sin is cured as you bring it out into the open and admit it. Confession says, "yes, that's what I did, that's what I'm like."

James puts the healing after the confession, and after the prayer. This requires being open with one another, admitting where we are spiritually, or where we are not, and praying for one another, for forgiveness and strength. How many times have you ever seen anything like this, where people talk to one another about their sin and pray?

In April of 1970, there was a revival at Asbury College in Wilmore, KY. The president, Dennis Kinlaw, said that it was basically public confession of sin and praying for one another.[48] There were no dramatic demonstrations of supernatural events like lightning, or people rolling on the floor in ecstasy. It was the Spirit of God putting His finger on sin in lives and people admitting that sin, and other people praying. The revival demonstrated the truthfulness of this verse.

The problem is not in finding forgiveness. The problem is in finding honesty. Have you ever admitted your sin to someone else in order to get them to pray for you? The promise of healing doesn't come until *after the confession*.

C. Healing from sin arises from the prayer of others. Of course we should confess our sins to God. That's where it all begins. But James wants us to go a step further and admit it to *someone else*. He's not interested in people holding up their dirty linen for all in the church to see. He wants us to confess to someone we know loves us enough to pray for us. It's confession because you want out of from the power of your sin. This is not a gossip session that satisfies the curiosity of those who delight to hear the dirt in other's lives. It involves people who seriously want to be holy and see holiness, and who will pray earnestly for the healing of a friend in sin.

Are you disconnected from someone? your father? Or mother? Or sister or brother? That's the effect of sin in your life. It may be your sin, your father's your mother's, but it is sin. And even if you think you are innocent in the situation, there is something you can do about the sin that crawls around on you. Go public and get someone else to pray.

You say, "I don't want anyone else to know about my secret sin; that would be embarrassing if someone knew what I was really like." No there is only one thing worse than someone finding out about your secret sin: *no one finding out about your secret sin*. That makes the secret stronger, which makes the deception stronger, which makes your hypocrisy greater. The blessing of confession is that you can once again be *honest*.

I remember the night our eldest son had a secret that he couldn't tell. He was sixteen, he was in great disobedience, he was in a terrible mood, and I said to him, "you are going to have to move out of this house." In escorting him out of the house, I was trying to tell him the possible places he could go at eleven pm. It suddenly struck me that my son was petrified. He wasn't showing the arrogance I expected, but rather panic.

Something was seriously wrong. At midnight we called a friend who was a good counselor and asked if we could come over to talk. The more the friend talked to him, the more we found out that he was under some sort of spell. At a party a week or two earlier he had been given a special name by a kid who was into witchcraft, a name that would give him great power, but also a name that he couldn't admit to anyone else. He was told that he would die when he shared the name. He had internalized that statement, "you will die when you admit this name," so that he was actually terrified at the prospect of admitting it.

It took more than an hour before he told us the name. But once he confessed that name, the control it had over him disappeared. He was relieved and everything was totally changed. Suppose that spell had continued in his life for years, that he had a name which he could not reveal. Imagine the damage that concept would have done.

That's what sin does. Do you want to live the rest of your life in sickness? Alone? Disconnected from the power and life of God? Why not be healed? It's connected with *admitting* your sin and getting praying friends to pray for you. You have to stop what you are doing, take off the mask, and humble yourself. Sometimes it's hard, sometimes so hard that we don't do it. We just keep trucking.

But you can be healed from the grip that sin has in your life. God will do it in response to the prayers of others.

IV. National sin calls for prayer

> *The effective, fervent prayer of a righteous man avails much.*
> *Elijah was a man with a nature like ours, and he prayed*
> *earnestly that it would not rain; and it did not rain on the*
> *land for three years and six months. And he prayed again,*
> *and the heaven gave rain, and the earth produced its fruit*
> *(James 5:16b-18).*

Elijah was an example of prayer's power. The power of prayer depends on earnest prayer. We can talk and sing about the power of prayer, but the power follows earnest prayer. The strange thing is that Elijah was *like us*. He had a nature *like ours*. He had the same problems and weaknesses we face. He got sleepy in prayer. He had emotional ups and downs. Sometimes he didn't feel like praying. And yet he brought about drought conditions for three and a half years.

Verse 16 calls Elijah "righteous." How could he be *righteous* when he was *like us?* Can we be righteous? The answer is *yes,* because Elijah was not some super monk-like person. He was normal, and normal people can be righteous. How? Some of the indications are in this passage:

A. They confess their sin, like verse 16 has just stated. Righteousness is not living without mistakes. It's *not tolerating them.* It wasn't that Elijah had conquered every last vestige of his problems but that he was fully in the fight against sin. He understood his own unrighteousness. "We do not present our supplications before You because of our righteousness but because of Your great mercies," Daniel prayed (9:18). Righteousness is ceaseless warfare against your own sins and weaknesses.

B. They have a passion for God's things. Elijah was bent out of shape because of Israel's sin. This was part of his warfare; not only his sins but those of his nation. He wanted God's will in the palace, he wanted to see God's glory in Ahab's government. We live in a world full of sin. How do you respond to that? The normal response is, *tsk, tsk.* Elijah's response was stronger. He wouldn't let the sin go on. I think he prayed this way: "Lord, You declared that You would take actions against Your people when they fell into national sin. Here is a nation doing exactly what You don't want them to do. Would You now do what You promised to do if they fell into sin?"

How did Elijah get to this state where he worried about the sin of his people? By confessing and forsaking his own sin. That's where the righteous part comes in. As he admitted his own sin and degradation, he began to see the danger of it in his nation. And he began to see the glory of forgiveness. We don't get beyond the *tsk,*

tsk state until we deal radically with our own sin. And what is radical? Admitting it, confessing and forsaking it.

C. They pray with seriousness. James says that it was "fervent prayer" (v. 16) and that he "prayed earnestly" (v. 17). He focused on prayer. The word, *fervent* means "wholeheartedness" and "seriousness of attitude." It represents someone who is getting desperate over the situation. Even the word *prayer* in verse 16 suggests seriousness. The word means "a petition, a request," even to the point of "begging." Elijah was begging God time and time again to do something about the sin of his people.

Have you ever prayed that way? We pray that way in emergencies, but do we pray that way over sin, like the abortion disaster in our country, or the marriage and family breakup with a huge percentage of our children grow up under only one parent? How about the church of Jesus Christ which seems to have the same dismal statistics in divorce and pornography and unfaithfulness? Is anyone bothered enough to plead with God over our country's downward slide?

D. Their requests are sin-centered. What was Elijah praying about? More money for his ministry? A larger house? Personal blessings? No, he was praying for the same thing James emphasizes in verse 16, the sin of his people. Ahab and Jezebel had introduced a new form of Baal worship, and things were going downhill quickly.

In Deuteronomy 28:23-24 God promised that He would make the heavens like bronze and change the rain to powder and dust when they turned from Him. Elijah was praying that God would fulfill His promise. He was intervening for Israel because he knew that they couldn't stay the same, they couldn't keep going the same direction. It would end up in total disaster. The three and a half year drought from the Lord was for the purpose of bringing the nation to a decision. It said, *wake up; it will only get worse.*

What are you praying for? New car? Nicer conditions? Freedom from financial burdens? Your retirement? Elijah was praying for repentance. He was overwhelmed by the sins of his people.

One man, by God's Grace, stopped a country in its tracks. Talk about terrorists bringing a country to its knees. Elijah brought a country to its knees *to bless it!* That's what God wants to do. Why doesn't God do this in America? Maybe no one has prayed like Elijah. Maybe people are responding to the sin around them with the *tsk, tsk* response. Maybe no one understands the danger of the growing cancer. All it took was one man to turn the nation around and bring healing.

Are you in sin? *You can't stay in it. You must confess and forsake it* **for your own good.** I plead with you to confess and forsake your sin, and get it out before it kills you. We're not talking about optional issues. You either get radical about sin, or it becomes a monster. And we need to get radical about the sins of others and pray for them that they will be healed.

We live in a country that may be worse off than Israel was in Elijah's day. We have been blessed immensely, just like Israel. But we have turned away from God to other gods. We are sinking every day into a morass of degradation. We kill our babies – without a second thought. We ruin our young people – without a moment of concern. Will someone rise up and pray like Elijah? You could do it. Interested?

Life situations should lead us to prayer. Sickness should lead us to prayer, sin should lead us to prayer, and national situations should lead us to prayer. Do you pray for these things?

V. Family problems call for prayer

Brethren, if anyone among you wanders from the truth, and someone turns him back, let him know that he who turns a

> *sinner from the error of his way will save a soul from death*
> *and cover a multitude of sins (James 5:19-20).*

This last section contains an unusual ending for a book of the Bible. James doesn't say *good-bye* or *peace be with you*. He gives no benediction or doxology. He simply ends on a note of saving a soul from death and covering a multitude of sins. It's almost as if he wants those words to ring in the listener's ears when the reader grows silent and steps down. "He does not wish any word or gesture of farewell to deflect our minds from this astonishing, terrifying, yet wonderful truth, that the fellowship we have as Christians is a fellowship of loving concern in which each of us is to act towards the other as God in Christ has acted towards us."[49]

This fact is one of the foundational pillars in the book, that as believers we are all in this together. James wrote as part of the family, to his brothers and sisters. No believer is an island. No one should ask like Cain, "am I my brother's keeper?" The proper answer is, "absolutely, and your sister too."

James commands, "Do not grumble against *one another*, brethren." Then he asks, "Is anyone *among you* suffering?" Then, "is *anyone among you* sick?" Then, "Confess your trespasses to *one another*, and pray for *one another*." Do you see other members of the family in these verses?

What does it mean to be in God's family? It means being in a fellowship of mutual concern. It means loving God by loving one another (1 John 4:11-12). And loving one another means much more than saying sweet nothings to each other at a church picnic. It goes so far as chasing brothers and sisters down to help bring them back to the joy of the truth. It's like Elijah who gave himself to prayer to rescue those he loved.

These two verses are still part of the *prayer* context. Families provide some of our greatest incentives to pray.

A. Families have trouble. We tend to view the concept of *family* with ideal pictures. We see children obediently sitting around the dining table, discussing theology or how they shared the gospel with the neighbor that day. Or asking questions about how the parents feel toward the liberal agenda, or the hypostatic union. As far as I know these pictures aren't matched by reality in any family on earth. Families are messy.

We think of movies like the *Sound of Music*, or *Cheaper by the Dozen*, and ask why our family is not like that. Then we hear well-meaning Christian leaders who suggest that if we do everything right, if we raise our children in the nurture of the Lord, they will never turn away. "After all," they say, "Proverbs says, 'train up a child in the way he should go, and when he is old he will not depart from it.'"

The danger is that the idealistic picture is discouraging for parents, especially when their children disobey and rebel. The result is a church filled with discouraged Christian parents who are positive they have messed up everything. The truth is that family trouble is *normal*. Problems surface to help children grow up. Growing up is almost always messy. Look at the messy things that are happening here:

1. One of the children is out of sync and moving in the *wrong* direction. *"If anyone among you wanders from the truth."* Don't be surprised. Don't think it is your fault. On the other hand, don't get proud over the fact that it's not you. This can be anyone, sometimes it is the very person you know will never have problems. But someone wanders from the truth. And this one is called a *sinner.*

All families have trouble. Adam and Eve were perhaps the best parents ever. They walked with God Himself in the cool of the evening and discussed their responsibilities. They were brilliant people. And yet, they had serious trouble. Son number one had an uncontrolled temper that led to murder of his brother. Anyone who thinks that when the parents do things right the children will all turn out fine doesn't understand the human heart.

But parents get hung up on ideal family pictures, so that when a child turns away from the Lord, the first question they ask is, "what did we do wrong?" The truth of the matter is that in spite of the fact that no parents are perfect, they may have done nothing wrong. At some point in life a child has to make up his or her own mind. And some of them, like Cain, turn against the best wisdom of their parents, and go their own way.

Exactly the same thing happens in the church. Even with the best pastor, the best teaching, the best fellowship, and the best examples in the church, people get strange ideas, and even turn away from the Lord.

What is a family to do in such a case? **Help him.** This section contains at least three examples of family help. In verse 14 the person *calls* the elders, in verse 16 the person *confesses* to someone else and asks for prayer. Here the brother or sister *goes out to help without permission*, simply because he sees a family member in need.

2. The result is projected to be serious. *"If anyone among you wanders from the truth."* This is more than not attending church or getting into an argument with an elder. We are talking about serious wandering. James uses words like, *multitude of sins, turns him, save a soul,* even *death*. He's referring to a direction in life that multiplies sins, like becoming a slave to sin and involving others.

What does James mean by *death?* The word described the end result of temptation back in 1:15. When yielded to, temptation produces sin, and full grown sin brings death. When Adam and Eve sinned in the Garden, they died, not physically, but they immediately died.

Their death was seen in their responses. They hid themselves from God, they realized that they were naked, and they suddenly possessed a fear of the presence of God. Their sin had instantly changed their relationship with God. Like the chop of a meat cleaver, their fellowship with God was severed.

That separation spread out in many directions, not the least in the fact that their firstborn son killed their second born son, resulting in physical death. Sin and death are always connected with separation of some kind. For an unbeliever, sin leads ultimately to eternal death, separated from God forever, in hell.

But even before that, sin separates. It ruins personal relationships in the family. People hide, like Adam and Eve did from the Father, people get angry with each other, like Cain and Abel, and that anger can lead to all kinds of disaster, including murder, as we saw in James 4 and 5.

In a real sense destiny is involved when people turn away from the Lord. That's why we are in the family. We make it as we make it together. "Our great concern must be to shepherd each other right through to eternity."[50]

The question becomes, "what is the family to do? what am I to do?"

B. God's solution to family problems is the *family*. We often think that God's solution is a specialist. After all, anyone who has turned away from the Lord needs professional help. But James says, "no, not necessarily."

1. Anybody can do the job. "*Someone turns him back.*" The word, *someone* is general and indefinite. Who? *It doesn't matter.* Maybe another family member, someone who sees the problem and is concerned enough about it to pray for wisdom and make a move to help. It's not talking about the senior pastor, or a ruling elder, or a deacon, or Sunday School teacher. Anyone who sees the need, even if they don't have a counseling degree, even if they haven't been to college, even if they haven't finished high school! The fact that God allows you to see someone else moving away from Him implies that He's giving you the opportunity and responsibility to step up and help.

You say, "I'm not qualified." How do you know? I would think that if you were not qualified you would be blind to what was happening. The fact that God has given you insight to see the deviation from the truth that others don't see, suggests that you are more qualified than you think.

It's like the parable of the Good Samaritan. What did it take to help this Jewish man? The priest and Levite could have done something to help, but didn't view a half dead man to be as important as their other responsibilities. This happens in a church where leaders are busy. What was needed to solve this man's problem? Anyone with just an ounce of compassion. Even a *Samaritan*, historically a national enemy.

Here's the point for each of us: *some of the greatest opportunities we will have to minister to others are cleverly disguised as inconvenient moves with insignificant people.* James started this thread back in 1:27 when he spoke of *visiting* widows and orphans in their distress. What's so hard about that? He went on to talk about the usher deciding *where to seat the poor man* in 2:3, and *one of you* deciding what to give to a brother and sister without food and clothes (2:16).

The question often is, "will you simply stop?" "Will you go across the room or next door to find out what's happening?" "Will you go over to visit or to help?" It's so easy to be like the priest and Levite, and keep walking.

2. The responsibility is to *turn* the brother back. The word "turn" is a word that means "to encourage or cause one to come back," or "to cause one to repent." This word describes our ministry to one another. We are seeking to *turn one another*.

That was John the Baptist's ministry. He had a "turning" ministry. We see it in the announcement of an angel to Zacharias his father: "Many of the people of Israel will he bring back to the Lord their God" (Luke 1:16). That word, *bring back* is this word, *turn*. It's the idea of bringing them back home, helping them get their mind off of whatever else has fascinated them, and re-introducing them to the privilege of family life with Christ.

Then the angel announced, "and he will go on before the Lord, in the spirit and power of Elijah, to turn the hearts of the fathers to their children and the disobedient to the wisdom of the righteous – to make ready a people prepared for the Lord" (Luke 1:17).

In order to prepare people for Messiah, John the Baptist needed to *turn the hearts of the fathers to their children*. What had happened? The nation was not prepared for Messiah because fathers had gotten away from their children. They had gotten busy with work, making money, or with their projects or sports, and had lost sight of their primary responsibility, to see *the raising of their children as their reason for being on earth*.

The result was a generation of children who did not know what family life was all about because their dads were absent, even though they may have been physically present.

Does that sound familiar? Perhaps you are the product of a dad who never turned to his children. He may have been rich, he may have provided you with many things, he may have been a big name in your neighborhood, but you grew up with something missing in your system, with a longing that he never met, a longing just to connect with his heart.

What happens if that father never wakes up? Apart from the Grace of God, you will live the rest of your life *compensating for that missing part,* that foundational assurance that is only laid down by parents. It adds a twist to your life and outlook so that you are always evaluating life in light of what your father never provided.

John the Baptist was not preaching about some optional addition that fathers should tack on to their lives. It was foundational. The hearts of the fathers needed to be turned – *or the entire nation would remain unprepared for Messiah!* In a similar way, Jesus' ministry was to turn people. In a similar way, our ministry involves turning people back to the Lord.

The truth is that *such wandering from the truth is not final*. We shouldn't accept their rebellious state as the final disposition of their lives. We should go after them to help.

C. The effort is of enormous benefit. *"let him know that he who turns a sinner from the error of his way will save a soul from death and cover a multitude of sins" (v. 20).*

Our culture has become overly cautious about a judgmental spirit. The idea seems to be that we can't judge anything today. People say things like, "judge not that ye be not judged." "Don't be too judgmental over those fourteen year old girls who need an abortion." "After all if there is no real right or wrong, who are you to set up yourself as the final authority?"

As a result we tend to shy away from invading other's lives to warn and turn them from what we know are going to be disastrous steps. We excuse ourselves with statements like, "maybe this is not the time," or "if he's a Christian the Holy Spirit will work in his heart," or "I'm not qualified." And we turn away from what could be our greatest ministry, *saving a soul from death* and *covering a multitude of sins.*

He will save a soul from death suggests that if he didn't make the move, the person would die. And *covering a multitude of sins* suggests that if things keep going without an interruption that turns the person, sin will sprout up in many places.

Saving a soul and covering multitudes of sins is not attributed to a preacher or professional, but to a person concerned enough to pursue a wanderer. It's a job that looks insignificant, like the shepherd who leaves ninety nine to go after the one, or father who leaves his other children to search for one. It may not look that important, but in the end it's value is enormous, covering many sins.

Who is going to help a wandering brother? *Someone with the heart of a mother or father.* Someone with the heart of a shepherd – who realizes that *this wandering brother or sister* **is my life!** That's what it means to be *like Jesus* because that's what He did.

D. Most of this kind of work is *unseen.*

1. Who knew that Elijah was praying fervently? He saw his brother, the nation of Israel, wander away from God. He gave himself to plead with God about the weather. God answered and blessed them with a drought, and turned the nation back to Himself through a series of miracles. What was the key to their *turn?* The marvelous preaching of Elijah? The force of Elijah's persuasive ability to turn them and make them think differently? No, Elijah stayed on his knees until God moved in the situation.

When our eldest son ran away and disappeared with our car, we prayed, until he was arrested 75 hours later. We first prayed in anger for his arrogant stupidity, then we prayed in fear for his life, then we prayed for God to rescue him from whatever situation he got into. But we prayed twenty four seven. He was always on our minds. I have thought many times since then about whether I have ever prayed that way for anyone else.

I'm convinced that Elijah prayed that way – in anger for Israel's arrogant stupidity, then in fear for their lives, then praying for God to rescue them from judgment he knew was coming. It's the unseen work of someone who understands the danger.

2. Who knew that someone was going after the wanderer alone? Nothing happened until someone decided to start praying and going after the wanderer. Jesus said, "if your brother sins, rebuke him; and if he repents, forgive him" (Luke 17:3). To "rebuke" someone you have to make a move. Call him. E-mail him. Go to his house. Write him a letter. Send him a gift. Ask him what you can pray for in his life. It all begins by interrupting your busy schedule to go after someone. It may be only a five minute visit, or a one minute phone conversation. But that's where *saving a soul from death and covering a multitude of sins* begins

You and I have the tremendous privilege of helping each other conquer sin. That's where community holiness develops. That's the heart of Jesus Christ, who gave His life to save a world of condemned sinners. Maybe that's why God saves His highest honors to those who rescue others. Daniel said: "Those who are wise shall shine like the brightness of the firmament, And those who turn many to righteousness like the stars forever and ever" (12:3). May we love enough to seek to turn others back.

ABOUT THE AUTHOR

James Samuel Schuppe was born and raised in a four-child Christian family in the Washington area. His father worked for the Post Office Department. He trusted Christ as Savior in 1949 when a neighbor took four or five kids on the block to a meeting he was holding at a church in Washington, DC. He entered the Washington Bible College in 1959 and then the Capital Bible Seminary in 1963, graduating in 1966. He then was offered a full-time position as instructor in speech at the Washington Bible College for the fall of 1966 and taught there for twenty-three years.

Jim and the former Martha Hearn were married in June 1970 at her father's church in Rossville, Georgia. They have been blessed with six children, fifteen grandchildren, and three great-grandchildren. In 1989 the family moved to Lynchburg, Virginia, where Jim taught at Liberty University for seven years. For a short time he served as interim pastor of Grace Church in Roanoke, Virginia.

He was invited to become pastor of Belcroft Bible Church in Bowie, Maryland, in 1996, and served there for sixteen years, retiring in 2012. He and Martha now live in Shepherdstown, West Virginia, and enjoy country life in "almost heaven." In addition to teaching and preaching, he enjoys family life, music, sports (with specialties in ping-pong and racquetball), carpentry and auto mechanics (Hondas only).

Bibliography

"2017 Fire Season." Fire.ca.gov/incidents/2017/.

William Barclay, *The Letters of James and Peter.* Philadelphia: Westminster Press, 1960.

Barclay, William. *A New Testament Wordbook.* New York: Harper & Brothers, no date.

Boyce, James. *Bible Studies Magazine.* 3/80, 5-8.

Brotherton, J. goodreads.com/quotes/284194-my-riches-consist-not-in-the-extent-of-my-possessions.

Bruce, F. F. *Commentary on the Book of the Acts.* Grand Rapids: Eerdmans Publishing, 1968.

Calvin, John. *Calvin's Commentary on the Bible.* https//www.studylight.org/commentaries/cal/james-2.html.

Chung, Frank. "How Jack Whittaker's life was destroyed by a $444 million lotto win." https//www.news.com.au/finance/money/wealth/how-jack-whittakers-life-was-destroyed-by-a-444-million-lotto-win/news-story/6691ac60ed1674e9e1c24e98a0cd3e96.

Copeland, Gloria. *God's Will is Prosperity.* Fort Worth: Kenneth Copeland Publications, 1978.

Dibin, Samuel. "Mahatma Gandhi and Christianity." *Christianity Today,* August 14, 2008.

Eareckson, Joni. *Joni, an unforgettable story.* Grand Rapids: Zondervan Publishing, 2001.

Fluet, Steve. "Local Triathlete Adds to Legend." https//www.ironman.com/triathlon-news/articles2003/11/.

Geisler, Norman. *Signs and Wonders.* Wheaton, IL: Tyndale, 1988.

Goode, Steve. "Growing up alone, unneeded." *The Washington Times,* January 8, 2006: B6.

Graham, Ruth Bell. *P.U.S.H. – Pray Until Something Happens!* https//www.godswordisflawless.org/PUSH%20Until%20Something%20H appens.html.

Guinness, Os. *The Call: finding and fulfilling the central purpose of your life.* Nashville: Word, 1998.

Hodges, Zane. *The Epistle of James.* Denton, TX: Grace Evangelical Society, 2009.

Jefferson, Thomas. "Quotation." Monticello.org/site/research-and-collections/honesty-first-chapter-book-wisdom.

Jeremiah, David, *The Handwriting on the Wall.* Dallas: Word Publishing, 1992.

Kinlaw, Dennis. *1970 Film of Asbury College's Revival.* https://www.archive.org/details/RevivalFilmOfThe1970RevivalAtAsburyColl egeInKentuckyUsa.

Lenski, R. C. H. *The Interpretation of The Epistle to the Hebrews and The Epistle of James.* Columbus: The Wartburg Press, 1946.

LeVee, Luella Nash. *Pure Joy, walking through trials with Christ.* Rockville: Cristus Books, 2003.

Lewis, C. S. *Mere Christianity.* New York: Macmillan, 1955.

Lewis, Joe E. brainyquote.com/quotes/joe_e_lewis_151200.

Mayor, Joseph. *The Epistle of St. James.* Grand Rapids: Zondervan Publishing, 1954.

McCoy, Terrence. "The homeless man who went to Harvard Law with John Roberts." *Washington Post,* July 13, 2015. https://www.washingtonpost.com/local/social-issues/the-homeless-man-who-graduated-from-harvard-law-school-with-chief-justice-john-roberts/2015/07/13/63257b5c-20ca-11e5-bf41-c23f5d3face1_story.html.

Motyer, J. A. *The Tests of Faith.* London: Inter-Varsity Press, 1970.

Muggeridge, Malcolm, *Christ and the Media*, Regent College Publishing, 2003.

Oesterley, W. E. *The General Epistle of James*. In "The Expositor's Greek Testament." Grand Rapids: Eerdmans Publishing, 1961.

Patterson, Ben. *Waiting – Finding Hope when God Seems Silent*. Downers Grove: InterVarsity Press, 1989.

Plummer, Alfred. *The General Epistles of St. James and St. Jude*. New York: A. C. Armstrong, 1905.

Ramsey, David. "Biggest-ever state lottery winner finally claims $177 million win." *Arkansas Times*, April 17, 2017.

Serrao, C. Jeanne Orjala. *James, A Commentary in the Wesleyan Tradition*. Kansas City: Beacon Hill Press, 2011.

Sterling, Joe, Sarah Sirgany and Ian Lee. "Egypt Cabinet OKs state of emergency after Palm Sunday church bombings. *CNN World, April 10, 2017*. https://cnn.com/2017/04/10/middleeast/egypt-church-explosion/index.html.

Smith, Logan Pearsall. http//www.brainyquote.com/quotes/logan_pearsall_smith_106830.

Sorgius, Kim. *Not Consumed Ministries*. https://notconsumed.com/cancer-is-the-best-thing-that-happened-to-me/.

Tada, Joni Eareckson. *When is it Right to Die?* Grand Rapids: Zondervan Publishing, 1992.

Thayer, Joseph Henry, translator. *Greek-English Lexicon of the New Testament*. Grand Rapids: Zondervan Publishing, 1962.

Thoughtco.com/work-2699023.

Vaughan, Peggy and James. *Beyond Affairs*. New York: Dialog Press, 2010.

Walters, J. Michael. *James*. Indianapolis: Wesleyan Publishing House, 1997.

Webster-dictionary.org/definition/work.

Wesley, John. "Notes on James." *John Wesley's Bible Commentary*. http://www.godrules.net/library/wesley/wesleyjam2.htm.

Wilson, Douglas. *Credenda Agenda.* Moscow, ID: Canon Press, Vol 6, Num 4.

Yancey, Philip. "Gandhi and Christianity." *Christianity Today*, April 8, 1983, 37.

Zodhiates, Spiros. *The Epistle of James and the Life of Faith.* Vol. 1, "The Work of Faith." Grand Rapids: Eerdmans Publishing, 1963.

Notes

1 Bruce, *Acts*, 64.

2 Hodges, *The Epistle of James*, 12.

3 Eareckson, *Joni, an unforgettable story*, 59.

4 Serrao, *James, A Commentary in the Wesleyan Tradition*, 52.

5 Levee, *Pure Joy*, 17. See also Kim Sorgius at notconsumed.com for a similar testimony from her eight year old son!

6 Thayer, *Lexicon of the New Testament*, 587.

7 McCoy, "The homeless man who went to Harvard Law with John Roberts."

8 Muggeridge, *Christ and the Media*, 25.

9 Motyer, *The Tests of Faith*, 38.

10 Goode, "Growing up alone, unneeded."

11 Childrenofzionvillage.org.

12 Dibin, "Mahatma Gandhi and Christianity."

13 Yancey, "Gandhi and Christianity."

14 Lenski, *Hebrews and James*, 567.

15 Calvin, *Notes on James 2*.

16 Guinness, *The Call*, 106.

17 Wesley, "Notes on James."

18 Webster-dictionary.org.

19 Thoughtco.com.

20 Barclay, *The Letters of James and Peter*, 94.

21 Plummer, *The General Epistles of St. James and St. Jude*, 172.

22 Fire.ca.gov., "2017 Fire Season."

23 Plummer, *op. cit.*, 175.

24 Plummer, *op. cit.*, 177.

25 W. E. Oesterley, *The General Epistle of James*, 454.

26 Jefferson, quotation.

27 Jeremiah, 175.

28 Peggy and James Vaughan.

29 *Tapeinophrosuna* in Thayer, 614.

30 Socrates, goodreads,com. Also attributed to Eleanor Roosevelt in "brainyquote.com."

31 *alazoneia,* Thayer, 25.

32 Ramsey, "Biggest-ever state lottery winner finally claims $177 million win."

33 Sterling, *et. al.,* "Egypt Cabinet OKs state of emergency after Palm Sunday church bombings."

34 Smith, brainyquote.com.

35 Barclay, *The Letters of James and Peter,* 136.

36 Motyer, *The Tests of Faith,* 100.

37 Chung, "How Jack Whittaker's life was destroyed by a $444 million lotto win."

38 Brotherton, goodreads.com.

39 Lewis, brainyquote.com.

40 Barclay, *A New Testament Wordbook,* 83.

41 *Ibid,* 84.

42 Walters, *James,* 189.

43 Patterson, *Waiting,* 14.

44 Tada, *When is it Right to Die?,* 173.

45 Fluet, "Local Triathlete Adds to Legend."

46 Thayer, *Lexicon of the New Testament,* 675.

47 Graham, *P.U.S.H. – Pray Until Something Happens!*

48 Kinlaw, *1970 Film of Asbury College's Revival.*

49 Motyer, *The Tests of Faith,* 126.

50 Motyer, *The Tests of Faith,* 125.

CPSIA information can be obtained
at www.ICGtesting.com
Printed in the USA
JSHW021244180422
25011JS00001B/4